D0684269

SPREAD YOUR WINGS AND FLI

SPREAD YOUR WINGS AND FLI

HOW TO EFFECTIVELY NAVIGATE COLLEGE AS A FIRST-GENERATION, LOW-INCOME STUDENT

JESSICA ILAYALITH MORA

NEW DEGREE PRESS

COPYRIGHT © 2021 JESSICA ILAYALITH MORA

SPREAD YOUR WINGS AND FLI

ISBN   978-1-63676-915-8   *Paperback*

          978-1-63676-979-0   *Kindle Ebook*

          978-1-63730-083-1   *Ebook*

Para mis abuelitos:

Manuel y Imelda Urquiza

Guadalupe y Luvia Mora

Y para mi famila de patojos:

Brandon, Ma, Pa, y Tony

CONTENTS

INTRODUCTION   **11**

PART 1.   **FRESHMAN YEAR**   **19**
CHAPTER 1.   YOU ARE NOT ALONE   21
CHAPTER 2.   WHO ARE WE LEAVING BEHIND?   31
CHAPTER 3.   THE FLI STUDENT EXPERIENCE   39
CHAPTER 4.   NO BLUEPRINT? NO PROBLEM   47

PART 2.   **SOPHOMORE YEAR**   **59**
CHAPTER 5.   ROCKING THE FIRST DAY OF CLASS   61
CHAPTER 6.   FINDING THE "YOU" IN COMM-YOU-NITY   73
CHAPTER 7.   HOW TO DEVELOP PERSONAL
RELATIONSHIPS   85

PART 3.   **JUNIOR YEAR**   **97**
CHAPTER 8.   STRIKING A BALANCE   99
CHAPTER 9.   NETWORKING AND HOW TO START   111

PART 4.   **SENIOR YEAR**   **131**
CHAPTER 10.   USING THE POWER OF SOCIAL MEDIA   133
CHAPTER 11.   BUDGETING AND PERSONAL FINANCE   149

PART 5.   PLANNING FOR LIFE AFTER COLLEGE   161

CHAPTER 12. FROM FLI STUDENT TO FLI PROFESSIONAL 163

CHAPTER 13. BECOMING A FLI GRADUATE STUDENT   173

CHAPTER 14. SPREAD YOUR WINGS AND FLI   181

ACKNOWLEDGMENTS   185

APPENDIX   191

I can do all things in Christ who strengthens me.

—PHILIPPIANS 4:13

INTRODUCTION

———

Crisp fall leaves crunched under Daniel as he walked around campus. The golden trees followed him as he strolled, the breeze gently grazing his sweater, offering him comfort. As a Texan who wasn't used to living in cold climates, he was making do with layering two sweaters. As he got deeper into campus, he felt the limestone buildings grow taller and taller, surrounding him in a cloud of whiteness and privilege. In that moment, he could not help but feel alone and isolated.

[handwritten margin note: cloud of whiteness]

It had already been a few weeks since he first set foot on campus, yet not once had he found someone who really understood him. He had hoped to find community among other Latinx students, but even among them he felt misunderstood. Yes, they shared a cultural background, but they seemed oblivious to what it meant to be a first-generation, low-income (FLI) student. After numerous missed connections between his classmates, he began to lose hope of ever finding a community on campus—one that would understand him without requiring an explanation.

As he made his way back to his dorm room, hands in his pockets, he sighed and resigned to make it through Northwestern as best he could. Slowly, the grandiose Northwestern arch poked its way through the trees, getting bigger with each step he took. He still remembered walking through the arch just a few weeks back, his family's wide smiles permanently sewn into his memory. Before he knew it, he reached the arch. He stood just below it, in a sliver of shade, as he waited for the walk sign to change.

Out of the corner of his eye, he could see a group of students hailing a cab. *How do these kids afford to take cabs all the time?* he thought. Yet just as the walk signed changed, something happened that would change his life forever. As the students all got into the cab, one student refused: "I can't take a cab! I'm QuestBridge. I can't afford it."

Daniel stood dumbfounded. Had he really found another QuestBridge Scholar—another student in the same scholarship program and one of the nation's largest networks of FLI students? Unable to contain his excitement, Daniel hurriedly caught up with the student. When he finally reached him, he was out of breath but could not hold back his question.

"Hey, man! Are you a Quest Scholar?"

"Yeah," the student answered, matter-of-factly.

Daniel's face lit up. "Me too! Do you know anyone else?"

"No. Do you?"

"No, me neither."

While they were both disappointed to hear they didn't know more members of the Quest community at Northwestern, they were ecstatic to have found each other. For Daniel, meeting another student like him was reassuring. For the first time since arriving on campus, he felt validated and understood.

Little did Daniel know that this friendship would be the catalyzing force Northwestern needed to make campus life more inclusive for students of underrepresented backgrounds. Eventually, this duo would advocate for a center for FLI students and create the largest QuestBridge Scholar chapter in the country. When Daniel was unable to find the community he needed to feel at home, he made his own family of FLI scholars.

Colleges and universities nationwide have become more focused on increasing socioeconomic and racial diversity on their campuses.[1] Yet in their rush to create a diverse environment, they have oftentimes overlooked what resources it might take for underrepresented students to succeed. First-generation, low-income students are one subset of students that have experienced this lack of support from their institutions, resulting in gaps in academic success across income brackets.

---

1 US Department of Education, "Fulfilling the Promise, Serving the Need: Advancing College Opportunity for Low-Income Students," March 2016.

Recent research on the topic has found that "while the graduation rate gap across race and ethnicity has been closing, the gender and income gap are still increasing over time."[2] What might attribute to an increasing gap in graduation rates? Harvard Professor Anthony Jack has found that a student's background, including cultural and social contingencies, can be crucial influences on how students experience college.[3]

Just because a FLI student arrives on a college campus does not necessarily mean they know how to take advantage of all the resources available to them. Even if all students within a university have "equal access" to resources and support systems, FLI students don't always know about them or how to go about asking for help. Gaining acceptance to college is only half the battle. The other half is making sure all students, especially underrepresented students, "experience a sense of community and a level of psychological well-being that contributes to their persistence to graduation."[4]

As a first-generation, low-income graduate from the University of Chicago, I have experienced some of these gaps myself. Unlike many FLI students, I graduated from a private high school on a scholarship, meaning, at least academically, I should have felt more prepared than my low-income peers.

---

2   Raj Chetty, et al., "Where is the Land of Opportunity: The Geography of Intergenerational Mobility in the United States," *Quarterly Journal of Economics*, 2014.

3   Anthony Abraham Jack, "Culture Shock Revisited: The Social and Cultural Contingencies to Class Marginality," Sociological Forum, 2014.

4   American College Personnel Association, "The 'Thriving Quotient': A New Vision for Student Success," May 2010.

In some regards, I was. I knew what office hours were. I had developed close relationships with my professors. I knew how to ask for help. Yet even with all of these tools in my toolkit, there were times where I felt unprepared for what I would face in college.

How could I tell my friends I couldn't go out to eat with them because I had to save money? How could I explain to my professor that I couldn't go to office hours because my work schedule conflicted with them? What's the difference between the bursar and the financial aid office? These questions were all on the top of my mind as I tried to balance academics, internships, and personal relationships. I couldn't be the only FLI student going through these issues at UChicago, let alone across universities nationwide.

In an effort to investigate this further, I decided to research the experiences of low-income students at elite institutions for my thesis on public policy. For my thesis research, I interviewed thirty low-income students at the University of Chicago to gain insight on their experiences regarding academic, personal, and professional development on campus. One of the most salient findings was that almost all students talked about feeling isolated and like an imposter, particularly during their first two years of college. During their first and second years, they did not feel like they were able to advocate for themselves, seek out the right resources, or find a sense of belonging on campus. Due to the structure of the public policy department, I ended my thesis with recommendations for UChicago to better serve the needs of students. These recommendations included:

1. Establishing an adequate transition during academic advisor turnover
2. Continuously asking for feedback from students on how to improve programming
3. Adding resources to ease the high-school-to-college transition for FLI students
4. Emphasizing community building among FLI students
5. Better advertising of FLI-specific resources to students

While I learned a lot in drafting these recommendations, I realized that sustainable and large-scale change would take years to implement. So what happens with FLI students now? As we wait for institutional change to come about, it's important that first-generation, low-income students today have the tools to succeed. It's not just about getting students to graduation and into the workforce; it's about ensuring students are able to thrive on a college campus and gain the social and professional skills that will prove invaluable in their adult lives.

My hope is that this book will help bridge some of those gaps. Whether you're going into a public or private institution, a four-year college or a two-year program, this book is aimed to help you learn how to navigate the college space and make it your own. It provides concrete steps you can follow to tackle topics, from going to office hours to finding your first post-grad job. It's all in here, tailored for you, by other former and current FLI students.

Inside, you will find stories from people with a variety of backgrounds. You'll hear from Jeff, an investment professional, now tackling what it means to be a person of color in a predominantly white corporate space. You'll also hear from Ana and how she went about creating QuestBridge. And you'll hear from numerous FLI professionals now working in the education sector to even the playing field for FLI student generations to come.

Whether you're an incoming college freshman or you're entering your senior year, there will be something in here for you. In no institution is being a FLI student easy, but you are never in this alone. I'm here. Jeff is here. Ana is here. And so many others are too. We are all here to pass along small nuggets of knowledge that we gained along our journey to hopefully make yours a little less bumpy.

This book is a compilation of stories and tips to help you make a home of your college campus, encompassing everything from academics to social and family life. You will learn what networking is and how to start building your own, how to read a syllabus and establish a relationship with your professors, and many other tips and tricks. I hope this helps. This is for you.

PART 1

FRESHMAN YEAR

CHAPTER 1

YOU ARE NOT ALONE

"No matter where you come from or how much money your family has, I want you to know that you can succeed in college, and get your degree, and then go on to build an incredible life for yourself."

—MICHELLE OBAMA[5]

As I began to unpack and settle in to my college dorm on move-in day, I felt like I was touching history. Walking around campus was like taking a walk back in time—a time where the cobblestone sidewalks and the gargoyles didn't seem out of place. As I walked, I passed the law school where Barack Obama had taught and the dorm where Bernie Sanders had stayed when he was an undergrad. History felt so tangible to me in that moment. I felt invincible.

I don't quite remember where I was or when it happened, but at some point during my walk of history I was bestowed a

---

5   Tina Tchen, "First Lady Michelle Obama: 'I'm First,'" *The Obama White House* (blog), February 5, 2014.

title. I was a FLI student. I was unclear as to what that meant. The word "FLI" seemed like a word other FLI students seemed really proud of and excited to talk more about. I would later learn that FLI stood for first-generation, low-income, and it represented students whose parents did not attend two- or four-year colleges and who were Pell Grant eligible.[6]

While the definition fit me like a glove, I was a bit taken aback by my new label of "low-income." Growing up, I never felt like my family was "poor." We lived in a nice apartment on the North Side of Chicago. I had my own bedroom and even got to go on vacation with my family every few years. Certainly these were not the characteristics of a "low-income" family. Little did I know, my perception of income would soon change.

Before I dive any deeper, I should disclose that while I did experience many challenges of being a FLI student in college, experiencing culture shock or navigating a predominantly white space were things I was familiar with before arriving at UChicago. In his research, Professor Anthony Jack reveals the existence of two types of low-income students: the privileged poor and the doubly disadvantaged. He describes privileged poor students to be those "who went to private high school, usually well resourced."[7] On the other hand, doubly disadvantaged students are those who went to a public and usually under-resourced high school.

---

6   The Community Initiative, "What is FGLI?," *Yale University*, 2020.

7   Lory Hough, "Poor, but Privileged," *Harvard Ed. Magazine*, 2017.

Yet even with having gone to a predominantly white and wealthy high school with many advanced classes, I still struggled in college. One of the biggest moments of uncertainty and doubt for me was when I took a chemistry class the summer before freshman year.

THE GAME OF CATCH UP

Chemistry... it's never been my strong suit. Any science, really. Something about the chemical structures, the math— it just doesn't stick with me. In the summer of 2016, however, I decided to give it a second chance. If I was going to be a computer science major when I started college in the fall, I needed to get as much of a head start as possible.

I remember heading into class that first day, excited. How hard could it be, really? This was college—my new beginning. The professor's introduction was brief. Name, pronouns, research interests. Right away, he dove into the formulas, balancing equations, and protons and neutrons. It was a hurricane of information coming at me faster than I could make sense of it all. There were brief flashbacks to material I learned during my high school chemistry class. It was like seeing a distant relative after years of not seeing them. I could recognize their face, but barely remembered anything about them.

I wrote down notes as fast as I could, but by the end of the class my page was flooded with question marks. As class wrapped up, I noticed many of my peers smile. They looked at each other, sharing in their happiness that this class would *only* be a recap of the AP Chemistry course they had taken the previous year.

I couldn't believe it. How was it that they were so prepared to be successful in this class, yet I was not? How did they even learn college level chemistry in high school, and how in the world was I supposed to catch up to them? It seemed impossible.

UChicago was meant for the smartest of the smart; maybe it was not meant for students like me. How was I supposed to get through four years at UChicago if the first class already felt like a game of catch up? Could I go to the professor for help? Would he think I was stupid for not being familiar with the material already? How could I go into office hours and ask for help on *everything*? The thoughts continued to race through my mind at speeds impossible for me to understand.

I decided then that my best option would be to go to a peer for help—one of those "I took AP Chemistry in high school" students—and hope for the best.

"Hey, want to study for Chemistry together?"

It seemed like a simple enough ask. He said yes. We scheduled a study session for the next day—more than enough time before our next problem set was due. The next day, we met in a library next to the dorms.

"This shouldn't take long," he assured me. What he didn't know was that the homework assignment was already burning a hole through my backpack. I hadn't been able to get a single problem done the night before.

We opened the textbook, heavy with problems that drew a deep line between my peer's knowledge and my own. Problem one: We wrote the equation in our notebooks. I stopped, staring at the jumble of numbers and letters on my sheet. He continued, jotting down notes and looking up the periodic table on his computer. Then he stopped, placing the pen in his mouth, deep in thought.

"What do you think?" he asked.

I gave up. I couldn't keep pretending like I knew what was going on. It was time to come clean. As I explained my limited background in chemistry and my recent frustrations in the classroom with him, I could feel the tears in my eyes. I needed so much help that I didn't even know where to start. When I was done, he closed his textbook and rapidly began typing something. I couldn't quite make out what he was typing, but within a few seconds a periodic table and a step-by-step process on how to balance an equation popped up on his screen.

"Let's work through this one together," he said encouragingly. He jotted each step down in his notebook and began explaining, stopping periodically to make sure I was following along.

After practicing a few of the same types of questions over and over again—many more times than I dare admit—I finally understood. I could practically scream from the excitement. I couldn't believe it! My mind felt like it had gone through an entire gymnastics class, tumbling, turning, tossing, until it finally nailed a move.

That night we only got through one problem, but the take-away was much greater. I realized that feeling alone in my room and not going to anyone for help was the greatest disservice I could've done for myself. A peer who barely knew me helped me understand an important concept, regardless of how long it took. If he was willing to do it, how much more willing would a professor or teaching assistant be?

Unsurprisingly, a version of the story above is experienced by many, if not all, FLI students. In his book, *The Privileged Poor: How Elite Colleges are Failing Disadvantaged Students*, Professor Anthony Jack describes how FLI students arrive at college campuses nationwide "scarred by poverty with all of its familiar ills, including a lack of social and academic preparation for college life."[8] In my experience, college was particularly hard, because I went from being a good student in high school to having to put in additional hours of studying to feel on the same page as my peers.

For this reason, it's important to recognize two things: (1) you are not alone in your struggle; and (2) self-advocacy is a must-have to be successful in college. While this book provides some tools and insights to help you navigate these incredibly tricky spaces, it is ultimately on you to take a chance and start putting things into practice. It will most certainly feel

---

8   Anthony Abraham Jack, *The Privileged Poor: How Elite Colleges Are Failing Disadvantaged Students* (Cambridge, MA: Harvard University Press, 2019).

uncomfortable or weird the first few times you put yourself out there, but I promise it will be worth it.

TWENTY SECONDS OF COURAGE

During my freshman year of high school I had a dean, Mr. Windus. The best way to describe Mr. Windus is that he was an incredibly kind soul who was always available to listen, offer advice, and lend a hand when needed. I remember going into his office and feeling like I belonged. Maybe it was the very comfortable couches or his wide array of books, but going into Mr. Windus's office always made my day.

On one of those days when I was procrastinating doing my homework and passing time sitting in his office, he very candidly asked me how I was liking high school. I said something along the lines of it's going well. I told him I loved my teachers, the cafeteria food, and I'd met another One Direction fan on the freshman retreat, so the first week truly could not have gone better. He smiled, happy to hear that I was doing alright.

It was then that he shared a wish he had for me. He said, "Don't ever let money get in the way of doing something you want."

When I first heard this, I was a little taken aback. As a student with a significantly lower income than most people at my private and predominantly white high school, I could list many ways in which money was preventing me from doing something I wanted. I left his office that day with that thought rolling over and over in my head. Then, it hit me.

More than a literal piece of advice, his wish was a mindset. He was pushing me to advocate for myself and ask for what I needed to be successful—in his example, *money*.

From that day forward, I was determined to not be afraid to ask for the financial support I needed. If I was running low on lunch money, I would ask the financial aid office for more. If my basketball coach was having us all buy basketball shoes for the season and I couldn't afford them, I would say so and ask if the school could pay for them.

I realize there is great privilege in going to a school that has the money to invest in their students. However, I think the lesson here is to take those twenty seconds of courage and not be afraid to be straightforward about what your financial situation looks like. You never know what resources might be available to help you.

During my junior year of college, my financial aid package decreased significantly to the point where I knew my family wouldn't be able to afford the expense. As a result, I went into the financial aid office, emailed my advisor, and eventually called the director of financial aid to see what could be done. I advocated for myself and leveraged people who could help me in an unfamiliar situation. I encourage you to do the same and embrace the attitude that Mr. Windus gave me that day. Find your voice and, wherever possible, *don't ever let money get in the way of doing something you want.*

Below is an action checklist to begin preparing for your freshman year. You've got this.

ACTION CHECKLIST

☐ Create a resource worksheet listing out the services available to you. Some must-haves on your list include:

  ☐ Your academic advisor
  ☐ Your career advisor
  ☐ Tutoring help
  ☐ Student health center
  ☐ Student counseling center
  ☐ Financial aid office
  ☐ Student support systems
  ☐ Student organizations
  ☐ University library (Always check if the library has your books before purchasing them yourself or if they might be able to lend you a laptop or other technology if you need it.)
  ☐ Local nonprofits and community partners

☐ How can you advocate for yourself? Make yourself three promises to support yourself when you get to college.

  ☐ Example 1: Make an appointment with your academic advisor to talk about your plans. If you don't know what you want to major in yet or don't know what classes to take, don't be afraid to say so and ask for guidance.

  ☐ Example 2: If there is an expense you can't cover yourself, ask your advisors if there is a university resource to help you out. Some resources universities may offer for FLI students can include a lending library, a laptop lending program, a micro-loan program, study abroad aid, and more.

☐ Example 3: Seek out staff that have experience advising and supporting FLI students specifically (your college might have structured mentoring programs, or you can always reach out to staff individually for help navigating a particular situation).

CHAPTER 2

WHO ARE WE LEAVING BEHIND?

———

"Dare to demand as much of your college as your college demands of you."

—ANTHONY ABRAHAM JACK[9]

For many first-generation, low-income students, arriving at a college campus is half the battle. Applying to college, scholarships, and financial aid all while attempting to get good test scores, grades, and the perfect concoction of extracurriculars can be a challenge for any student, but particularly for those coming from low-income backgrounds. In this chapter I will set the scene for what the higher education landscape looks like, why so many FLI students are left behind, and what college campuses are doing to increase both access and inclusion to their spaces.

---

9   Julie Deardoff, "Tony Jack on Diversity: 'Access Ain't Inclusion," *Northwestern University, School of Education & Social Policy,* October 29, 2019.

FINANCIAL BARRIERS TO ENTRY

Recent research has found that college enrollment levels across income brackets have been increasing across the board. In the midst of this increase, however, there are still significant gaps when comparing college enrollment across income levels.

One study analyzing the college student journey found that while "81 percent of high income high school graduates immediately [enroll] in college [...] [only] 52 percent of low-income students [do]."[10] With only 52 percent of low-income students immediately enrolling in college, it becomes apparent that there is something preventing this student population from even arriving on college campuses in the first place. One main factor deterring students from enrolling is their financial situation.

This was the case for Lyric Swinton, a Columbia, South Carolina native. As the eldest daughter of three, Lyric always knew she would have to be the one to carve the path for her and her sisters. She worked tirelessly for many years, joining multiple extracurriculars and earning the grades and test scores required to gain acceptance to a top university. Throughout her high school career, she was so focused on gaining a college acceptance that she didn't even think about what she would do if she actually got in.

---

10 American Academy of Arts and Sciences, "Getting into College," *A Primer on the College Student Journey, American Academy of Arts and Sciences*, September 2016.

In March of her senior year she was accepted to the University of South Carolina (USC). The joy of her acceptance was short-lived, however, when she realized her family had no way to pay for her undergraduate education. Four years at USC would come with a hefty price tag. Determined to make it work, Lyric sought out various scholarships and financial aid programs, eventually landing the Opportunity Scholars Program Scholarship, an award aimed at "[supporting] students in obtaining the education and skills needed to earn a career-focused, technical degree, and embark on a pathway to a successful career."[11]

Scholarship programs like the Opportunity Scholars Program are essential in making spaces of higher education accessible for FLI students and lowering barriers to entry into these otherwise elite spaces.

THE GAP IN SOCIAL CAPITAL
For students like Lyric who are able to find the financial support to get through college, their challenges are far from over. As a matter of fact, students coming from high-income families are three times more likely to attend college than their lower-income peers and more likely to succeed once they're on campus.[12] Researchers have attributed cultural

---

11   Central Piedmont Community College, "Opportunity Scholars Program," *Opportunity Scholars Program, Central Piedmont Community College*, 2020.

12   Raj Chetty, et al., "Where Is the Land of Opportunity? The Geography of Intergenerational Mobility in the United States," *National Bureau of Economic Research*, January 2014.

and social contingencies as potentially contributing to the way students experience class marginality.[13]

In other words, when FLI students arrive on college campuses they usually come from under-resourced high schools and are laden with family responsibility and a lack of cultural and social capital—the networks, resources, and knowledge—to navigate certain spaces. As much as these students would like for college to be a "clean slate," it is nearly impossible to feel a sense of belonging on college campuses without addressing the background students are bringing with them. Subsequently, FLI students end up "being surrounded by so much concentrated wealth and privilege [making] them feel alienated and confused—and sometimes plain mad."[14]

Lyric remembers arriving to campus and realizing that being a first-generation college student meant that she was "pulled out of [her] old life and thrown into a whole new life where [she] didn't really know anybody and [she had to] form an almost entirely new identity."[15]As Lyric began to craft this identity at USC, she observed that there was an increasing gap between the things her white peers knew how to do and the things she knew how to do. They knew successful interview hacks, how to network, and how to decipher what "business casual" meant. She did not. She didn't even own a

---

13   Anthony Abraham Jack, "Culture Shock Revisited: The Social and Cultural Contingencies to Class Marginality," *Sociological Forum,* 2014.

14   Paul Tough, *Years That Matter Most: How College Makes or Breaks Us* (Chicago: Houghton Mifflin Harcourt, 2019), 108.

15   The Patchwork Feminist, 11, "First and Foremost," by host Lyric Swinton, aired November 2019 on Garnet Media Group.

blazer for formal occasions until her junior year when she finally got her first pant suit.

Lyric was confronted first-hand with this gap in social knowledge and financial power while working as a hospitality attendant at the USC stadium. She shares her experience in her TED Talk, describing how she realized that she and her peers were on unequal footing when it came to their undergraduate experience. "Many of my colleagues sat there with their families and even though during school hours we were equals, in this space I was making a little over minimum wage amongst my peers that were sitting in seats that were worth thousands."[16]

Here she points to the fact that while her undergraduate experience involved her juggling academics and work, her peers only had to worry about academics given that their families were taking care of their financial wellbeing. While she and her peers were studying at the same institutions, their experiences couldn't be more different.

WHERE THIS BOOK COMES IN

While a bachelor's degree used to be seen as a way to climb up the socioeconomic ladder, now it is commonly seen as an insurance policy against downward mobility. A study conducted of graduating students at Ivy League universities and similarly prestigious institutions found that between 10–16

---

16 Lyric Swinton, "What I Have Learned as a First-Generation College Student," filmed December 5, 2018 at TEDxUofSC, Columbia, SC, video, 1:51-2:04.

percent of students were able to achieve at least some economic mobility after graduating.[17] For low-income families, this economic mobility is seen in an average of $335,000 to their lifetime earnings.[18]

While this is a book for first-generation, low-income students and how they can effectively navigate college campuses, I should note that I believe the work of making college campuses more inclusive and supportive of FLI students falls on institutions themselves. It is not enough to just provide financial support to students—although that is definitely an important step. FLI students require additional resources and support systems in order to thrive on campus. Emphasis and priority should be placed on *both* graduating and having an exceptional college experience.

Across college campuses nationwide, FLI students are advocating for the university resources they need to be successful. This includes asking for academic advisors specific to first-generation students, creating cultural centers on campus, and pushing for cultural sensitivity training for professors and faculty. While specific policies vary from institution to institution, the overarching goal is to make college campuses more inclusive to students of color and other marginalized student populations.

---

17 Gregor Aisch, et al., "Economic Diversity and Student Outcomes at the University of Chicago," *The New York Times,* January 18, 2017.

18 Paul Tough, *Years That Matter Most: How College Makes or Breaks Us* (Chicago: Houghton Mifflin Harcourt, 2019), 256.

While this broader institutional change happens, this book is here to guide students and provide them with some resources to be successful on their campus. Hopefully in the coming years, colleges will offer FLI students enough of the academic, career, and social resources they need to succeed that this book will become useless. That is my dream for the future.

CHAPTER 3

THE FLI STUDENT EXPERIENCE

"Tell the story of the mountain you climbed. Your words could become a page in someone else's survival guide."

—MORGAN HARPER NICHOLS[19]

BUT FIRST, A STORY...

Just imagine: It's 8 p.m. on a Friday. You're about to settle into your pajamas and grab a glass of wine when your phone screen lights up. For a second you think it might be your crush and your heart skips a beat. No, it's not your crush; it's your friend Luisa. She is inviting you over to her house. Your friends are all there and they're having a game night. You promised yourself you would try to go out more and really exercise that extrovert muscle, but real exercise might be

---

19 Leighann Blackwood, "14 Encouraging Life Quotes from Writer and Artist Morgan Harper Nichols," *Medium*, August 29, 2019.

better than having to get dressed and head over. Nevertheless, you push yourself out the door and get in the car.

The night is calm—too calm. You wonder if the entire city has chosen to have a Friday night in. Maybe you should have stayed in too? After a bit of driving you arrive at Luisa's house. She's left a spot open in her driveway for you. You haven't even gotten to the door yet when she's already opened it.

"Jess! Come in! We're just about to start another round."

As you head inside, you pour yourself a glass of wine and sit down with everyone else. You look at the coffee table everyone is sitting around and see that there are tiny silver figurines on the table. There's a silver turtle, a coin, a mini replica of the Eiffel Tower, a tiny silver pencil, and many more objects you can't quite make out. Everyone seems to have some assortment of these tiny silver pieces in their hands along with seven plain wooden blocks. Luisa hands you a red solo cup with your own assortment of silver pieces and your own seven wooden blocks.

"Ready?" she asks.

Just as you're about to ask her what game they're playing and what the rules are, someone yells "Go!" Your friends stare intently at their blocks. Some decide to stack them, while some simply form figures on the ground. After a few minutes you see someone taking the silver pieces and running to place them in different parts of the house. Slowly, everyone starts doing the same.

Meanwhile you are still on the ground in a circle of wooden blocks and silver pieces trying to figure out what you're supposed to be doing next. While you're trying to have fun with it, you begin to get frustrated. How are you supposed to play the game if you don't know the rules?

WHAT THE RESEARCH SAYS

Higher education has the potential to award opportunities to lower income students and help them climb the socioeconomic ladder. If students can adequately profit from the resources available at their institutions, college can be an engine of social mobility.

However, the current state of higher education serves as "an obstacle to mobility, an instrument that reinforces a rigid social hierarchy and prevents them from moving beyond the circumstances of their birth."[20] While it is impossible to believe that a book can reverse the limitations of centuries of discriminatory practices, my hope is that this book will offer some insights into the world of higher education so that FLI students go in fully knowledgeable of the kind of space they are walking into.

First of all, some of the nation's oldest colleges were founded in the 1600s. The United States looked a lot different than it does now. As a result, colleges and universities nationwide have struggled to make their campuses feel welcoming to marginalized students, including, but not limited to, students

---

20 Paul Tough, *Years That Matter Most: How College Makes or Breaks Us* (Chicago: Houghton Mifflin Harcourt, 2019), 19-20.

of color, first-generation students, low-income students, and immigrant students.

Based on his continued research in the education field, especially on the first-generation, low-income student experience, Harvard Professor Anthony Jack has found that college campuses continue to be "bastions of wealth, built on the customs, traditions, and policies that reflect the tastes and habits of the rich."[21] For this reason, it is no surprise that FLI students struggle to adapt to the academic and social environments at college campuses. Institutions of higher education were not meant to serve this population of students, and therefore they are not always equipped with the tools to help these students be successful.

For many first-generation, low-income students, their college experience goes precisely like the story outlined above. They arrive on campus without knowing the "rules." Many of them have never seen a syllabus before or know what office hours are and how they work. They don't know what networking is or how to do it. While they try to get acclimated to the new academic and social environment they now find themselves in, they also have to figure out how to navigate the financial aid and bursar office and who to reach out to when they need help.

One of the areas that first-generation, low-income college students struggle the most in is communication and developing

---

21   Anthony Abraham Jack, "For Students Who Grew Up Poor, An Elite Campus Can Seem Like a Sea of Wealth and Snobbery," *Quillette,* August, 24, 2019.

academic and professional relationships in college. The expectation in college is that students are avid communicators about their needs and stellar advocates for themselves. They should be going in to office hours frequently in every class and working at developing relationships with their professors.

Beyond their role as teachers, professors are meant to be an additional resource in the college journey who can help with anything from finding research and internship opportunities to writing letters of recommendation or serving in a mentorship role. Being a professor in a classroom is only one part of their role. Yet many FLI students never learn this or if they do, they learn it during their junior or senior year of college, at which point it may be too late.

For many incoming FLI students, "trying to figure out when, how, and even why personal connections are needed can paralyze them, expanding the gap between them and their professors. It undercuts their sense of belonging."[22] For this reason, it is important to decipher the code of expectations for students before they even get to campus so that they can prepare for what college will be like and excel accordingly. Consider this a handbook to guide you through some of these unspoken expectations to help facilitate the high-school-to-college transition and ensure that you feel like you have the tools to navigate any situation that might come your way.

---

22   Anthony Abraham Jack, *The Privileged Poor: How Elite Colleges Are Failing Disadvantaged Students* (Cambridge, 2020), 81.

MICHELLE'S STORY

Michelle arrived at Princeton University by car in the fall of 1981. Her father and boyfriend at the time dropped her off in front of her dorm and sent her off with well wishes for the start of her undergraduate career. From the first time she got to campus she had to learn to adjust to various aspects of campus life, especially on what it meant to be surrounded by extreme privilege and affluence.

Michelle describes being surrounded by students who had come from rigorous prep schools that had prepared them for college life. On the other hand, "[she] didn't even know the language of college, including what a syllabus was."[23]

The Michelle in this story goes by Michelle Obama now, but at the time, she was just Michelle. Her story proves how common it is to struggle acclimating to the college environment, yet eventually find your footing. During her first year, the unfamiliarity of college became especially tangible to Michelle when it came to the academic and social culture at Princeton. One moment that symbolizes this unfamiliarity for her is when she didn't know what sheets to buy for her bed. As a result, her bedsheets ended up being too short and she ended up having to sleep "with [her] legs sticking out past the end of the sheets" for the entirety of her freshman year.[24]

---

23 ABC News, "From Michelle Obama's humble Chicago upbringing to the White House: Part 1," YouTube, November 11, 2018.

24 Tina Tchen, "First Lady Michelle Obama: 'I'm First,'" *National Archives and Records Administration*, February 5, 2014.

It is precisely moments like these that Michelle uses to encourage first-generation students not to give in to their feeling of not belonging. She, herself, knows firsthand what it feels like not to feel that immediate sense of belonging and community and, in fact, struggled with that throughout her freshman year.

Yet after a few years at Princeton, she began to realize her insecurities were all in her head and she was just as smart and capable as every other Princeton student. As soon as she made this mental switch, her mindset shifted from surviving in college to thriving. As a flourishing college student, Michelle became an expert on building relationships both inside and outside of the classroom. She became a bold student and one who was not afraid to step outside of her comfort zone. She found that it was easiest to make friends and find a support network when she put herself out there and took risks.

Unlike middle school or high school, Michelle realized that college is the time when you've got to advocate for yourself the most and realize that while you may encounter challenges along the way, you've got what it takes to succeed. Based on her experience, she encourages students to "ask for the help [they] need… and reach out early and reach out often."[25]

---

25 Frances Bridges, "Michelle Obama Shares Advice with First-Generation College Students At Beating The Odds Summit," *Forbes*, July 24, 2019.

CONCLUSION

From their origins, colleges and universities in the US were not made for a diverse student population. Consequently, it is no surprise that low-income, first-generation, and students of color have such difficulty navigating a space built on a completely different set of values than they are used to. Even students like Michelle Obama can vividly recall the challenges they had to go through and the mindset shifts they overcame in order to graduate from a predominantly white institution.

In order to help you feel less of an imposter in the new university you will call home, I have outlined a few actionable items for you to tackle life on campus.

ACTION CHECKLIST

- ☐ Make a list of the resources your college offers specifically for FLI students.
- ☐ Make a list of on campus communities you want to seek out and be a part of.
- ☐ Make a list of terms you are unfamiliar with to ask your academic advisor when you first meet.
  - ☐ Some examples can include: office hours, syllabus, networking, LinkedIn, etc.
  - ☐ When you don't know what a particular major or minor is, also feel free to ask your advisor. I didn't know what "Public Policy" was until my second year of college!

CHAPTER 4

NO BLUEPRINT?
NO PROBLEM

———

"Upward mobility is not simply a question of earning more money than one's parents. It is also, for many people, a process of cultural disruption: leaving behind one set of values and assumptions and plunging into a new and foreign one. It can be disorienting and emotionally wrenching, shattering family ties and challenging deeply held notions of identity and purpose."

—*PAUL TOUGH*[26]

Landing in LAX the summer of 2019, blasting "Party in the USA" on my headphones, I felt it in my soul that this was going to be an exceptional summer. That summer I had an internship lined up with an investment management company in downtown Los Angeles. Yet in the midst of all of the

———

26 Paul Tough, *Years That Matter Most: How College Makes or Breaks Us* (Chicago: Houghton Mifflin Harcourt, 2019), 10.

excitement, doubt couldn't help but sneak its way into my mind. As someone with a health research background and zero investment knowledge, I was unsure what the summer would hold for me.

During my first week on the job, names, job titles, and acronyms flew past me like darts being thrown at a board. Some stuck in my mind, others landed way off the mark. One name that stuck with me was Jeffrey Garcia, a successful investment analyst at the company. I heard that he was heavily involved in a charter school network in LA and was incredibly passionate about immigration rights and giving back. How was it possible for these passions to coexist with a life in corporate? Needless to say, from that first week, I knew Jeff was someone I needed to get to know.

It was almost two months later that I finally scheduled time to talk with him. I met him at his office and we walked over to a coffee shop just across the street. We had originally scheduled a twenty-minute coffee chat, yet very easily, we exceeded that time, talking about everything from must-visit places in LA, to our families both being from Michoacán, Mexico, and our mutual interest in educational advocacy. While Jeff and I bonded over a shared language and cultural heritage, what struck me most of all was our shared FLI background.

Talking to Jeff that day reminded me that, in predominantly white spaces, just one small connection can mean the world. After almost an hour of talking to him, I realized that the Jeff sitting in front of me—a successful investment analyst at a top firm—was not always sure of his career plans, nor was he always so fluent in how to successfully navigate a predominantly white space.

A FAMILY PROMISE

Jeff still remembers the promise he made to himself when he was a kid. It was the mantra that got him up in the morning to go to school even on the days when he had stayed up a little too late. He would repeat it to himself over and over again on his way to school: *I am going to get the best job and career I can so I can help my family financially.* It was a tough legacy to fulfill, especially for an eight-year-old boy. At that age, Jeff didn't know what the "best" job was, but he knew he was good at math. As he grew older, he realized that engineering might be a good field for him.

When Jeff arrived on Stanford's campus as an undergraduate, he had his mind set on becoming an engineer. Even as a first-year student, he had already outlined his pathway to success. He knew he had to excel academically and participate in various extracurriculars, just as he had in high school. However, there was one part of the puzzle that he wasn't familiar with. How did one go about landing the best summer internships and a well-paying job after college? That was a question that was drilled in his mind as he navigated Stanford's campus.

ENCOUNTERING CULTURE SHOCK

Coming into college, Jeff participated in a summer program run by Stanford's School of Engineering. The program was designed for underrepresented students, many of whom included people of color, women, and first-generation, low-income students. When Jeff described the program to me, he emphasized that it had given him "a good understanding of what Stanford was about. It was very focused on the engineering curriculum [and] the broader mission from Stanford like how they approach undergraduate education and what resources are available." Through the month-long preorientation program, Jeff began building a roadmap for what it would take for him to be successful as a Stanford student.

Jeff's original plan upon moving to campus in the fall was to keep his head down, never talk to professors or advisors, and study and work hard to get through college—a common strategy for many FLI students unfamiliar with the expectations that await them in college. It was how he had always done things, and they had seemed to work for him thus far. A few weeks into college, however, he realized that simply doing the work was not enough to get the most out of his experience. In order to gain insight into what it would take to be a successful student at Stanford, Jeff became involved with El Centro Chicano y Latino, Stanford's Latinx community center.

At the center, Jeff was gained exposure to upperclassmen who could share expertise about student life. It didn't take him long to realize how valuable the information shared in these spaces could be. At El Centro Chicano y Latino, upperclassmen would volunteer information about navigating majors and professional opportunities even without him asking. All he had to do was listen to the advice and the resources they were offering.

"Hey! You could do research over the summer through this opportunity."

"If you want to work in engineering, you can do anything."

"If you want to think about business, consider this resource."

"If you want to get a PhD, there's a million ways to get there."

As he heard from more and more upperclassmen, he realized that there wasn't one "right" career for him to take and that asking for feedback or bouncing ideas off of someone wasn't so bad. There was so much left for him to learn during his time in college.

With the new advice in hand, Jeff began to uncover the opportunities that Stanford had to offer. He showed up for information sessions even if they were only meant for juniors and seniors. Jeff remembers going to the first few sessions thinking to himself, "I don't even know what these things are. But they're doing them so I'm going to go to the sessions and learn about [the opportunities] early." The more info sessions he attended, the more he learned about his own career interests and how he could cater Stanford's resources to his advantage.

WHO DO YOU WANT TO BE?

College is a time when you have to make numerous big decisions about what you want your life to look like. If you want to go to med school, you need to get on the pre-med track freshman year to start tackling your pre-med requirements.

If you want to eventually apply to a PhD program, you'll probably want to start getting involved in research on campus. For Jeff, his pathway wasn't as clear as being pre-med or pre-law. When he was considering what to major in or what internships to take, he was forced to take a step back and reflect on what his values were and how they could align with post-graduate opportunities.

His train of thought and self-questioning went something like this: "I care a lot about helping my parents. Why do I care about that? Well, it means that I really care about social justice and trauma. What's something that can help me reach my career and financial goals with my social justice passion in mind?"

There wasn't automatically a right answer to these questions. First, Jeff tried out a fellowship with the Haas Center for Public Service, where he got to work with a nonprofit in Los Angeles the summer after his freshman year. While a job in the nonprofit sector didn't necessarily align with his goal of making a lot of money, he really enjoyed the experience. Jeff told me about his involvement at the nonprofit.

He said, "I learned how to work in an office, I cared a lot about public health and underprivileged neighborhoods, and I was passionate about social justice."

After that summer he began trying out jobs in the corporate sphere to see how he would like them. He took internships at places like JP Morgan and NBC Universal. Jeff knew this was a route that aligned with his values of helping his family financially.

After trying out both corporate and nonprofit environments, Jeff realized he had a choice to make. At Stanford, students with interests similar to his went down the nonprofit and public policy route. Regardless of what students were majoring in, Jeff knew that those who were passionate about social justice typically went into law or public policy. These careers, he thought, would both align very well with his value of giving back and advocating for underserved communities. But was it the best place for him?

Through lots of recruitment during the academic year, Jeff landed multiple summer internships in finance and business. He took advantage of the opportunities and translated them into full-time job offers after college. After weighing his options, Jeff realized that he couldn't walk away from the learning opportunity and financial benefit presented before him.

While in that moment he decided to go completely corporate, Jeff promised himself that he would bring his passion for social justice with him in the professional sphere. He realized many FLI peers were drawn to nonprofit and public policy. And he was left wondering: *Who is bringing social justice values to the corporate sector?* Jeff decided to take his passions for education access and immigration and continue working toward those causes while being on a business career trajectory. It was an opportunity that would support his childhood goals of helping his family, and, at the same time, bringing his values to the corporate sector seemed to be a path that was underexplored and worth pursuing to complement all the great work being done by his FLI peers.

Now, in addition to his full-time job as an investment analyst, Jeff also holds numerous board positions. He is on the Board of Directors of Value Schools, a charter school network in the Los Angeles area. He is also a board member for the Mexican American Legal Defense and Educational Fund, as well as a board member for Teach for America. While Jeff didn't always know what field he wanted to work in or how he would get there, he has now reached the balance of financial success and community involvement that he always dreamed of having.

YOU ARE ENOUGH. YOU HAVE ENOUGH TIME.

It's easy to look at someone like Jeff and think he always had it together, but during his undergrad years, Jeff was just like you and me. He didn't always have all the answers. The future seemed blurry at times. If you feel like you don't have a blueprint for how you want your college career to go from where you stand today, don't worry. If Jeff could go back, he would reassure his college self that things would be okay and would turn out well in the long run. He would approach freshman year Jeff, sit him down in El Centro Chicano y Latino, and say to himself, "Jeff, you are enough. And, Jeff, you have enough time."

When you are a first-generation college student, there are times where you can feel like college is the one shot you have to make it big. For many, it feels like the weight of your family—the weight of the world—is on your shoulders. If you're not taking care of yourself, this pressure can very quickly lead to mental health and physical issues. When you are feeling like this pressure is too big, take a deep breath, ask for help, and lean on your support systems to help you out. Your support system can be your family, but it doesn't always have to be. It doesn't even have to be a big support network. Developing even one, deep, and personal friendship or mentorship can make all the difference for many FLI students

And remember:

> *You are enough. You have time.*
> *You've got this.*

NO BLUEPRINT? NO PROBLEM.

Before I even set foot on UChicago's campus, I was already set on becoming a computer science major. Growing up I had always heard my mom say that tech was where the money was. The conclusion was clear: If I wanted to make good money, I *had* to major in computer science. When I sat in my first-ever computer science class my second year of college, I felt ready. I was in the front row right in front of the professor. My pencil and notebook were on my desk, reaching beyond the confines of the desk. I was ready to kick ass. While I don't remember much from that first class period, I do know I walked out feeling pretty confident. *How hard could it really be?*

As I sat down in one of the armchairs in Harper, one of UChicago's libraries known not to have any books, and pulled up my problem set, my heart sank. Up until that point I thought I had understood the material—maybe not 100 percent, but definitely enough to know where to ask for help. Boy, was I wrong. The problem set could be in Chinese for all I knew. I didn't even know what the first step was.

Unfortunately, that wasn't the last problem set I felt completely lost in. That entire quarter I felt like I was sinking, struggling to even come up for air. I felt like I was facing an existential crisis. Deep down, the answer was clear: there was no way I could be a computer science major. But then an even greater revelation came. *If I wasn't a computer science major, then what would I be?* I wasn't sure. After talking to my academic advisor about possible major changes and spending hours scrolling through the college catalogue, I still couldn't find a major that felt right.

It wasn't until my boyfriend at the time pulled out the different majors and their respective requirements on his computer and we started looking through options together that I found some hope. Unlike me, he had a four-year plan drafted from the moment he stepped on campus. If there was anyone who could help me choose a new major it would be him. As I talked to him about wanting to try out the History, Philosophy, and Social Studies of Science and Medicine major, I could see his face suddenly light up.

"You think I should do it?" I asked looking for reassurance.

"It definitely sounds cool and you could try a class out next quarter." He paused. I could tell he was up to something.

"How about Public Policy?" he asked, turning the computer around for me to see all the classes.

I couldn't believe it. It really looked like the perfect major. I could take a combination of economics, education, law, and statistics classes, and they would all count for the major. I nearly jumped for joy. As I sat in on my first Public Policy class, I was nervous. What if I didn't end up liking it? Would I have to stay an extra year if I didn't choose a major this quarter? My worries were wiped away as the professor began the class talking about the role of politics in US life. For the first time, I felt like I was exactly where I needed to be.

College is a compilation of the above moments. There are times where you feel so on a roll, like you couldn't see yourself doing anything else. When you feel that way, rejoice and enjoy those positive emotions. Similarly, there are moments where you feel like things are falling apart, like what you thought to be true are no longer true for *you*. That's okay too! In those moments, take a step back and recalibrate. What is going well for you? What could be going better? Are there any resources you could take advantage of or people you could talk to for help?

College is a transformative experience. It's silly to think that the person you were when you entered college is going to remain the same over the years. It's perfectly okay to switch majors, change opinions, and explore pathways you hadn't considered before. For this reason, don't be afraid to take advantage of preorientation programs. They help guide you in college life so that when you actually get to campus you can focus on discovering yourself, meeting new people, and finding your place.

ACTION CHECKLIST

☐ Apply to at least one preorientation program that your university has, especially if it's catered to first-generation, low-income students.

☐ Assess what career interests you have right now. Make a list of what you value about these careers. How can you begin to explore opportunities that will allow you to either confirm or recalibrate your interest?

☐ Make a list of three majors that sound appealing to you. Under each major, write down what you like about them. Compare these with your career interests. Do they align?

    ☐ Meet with your academic advisor to see what your tentative college schedule would look like if you pursued these majors.

PART 2

SOPHOMORE YEAR

CHAPTER 5

ROCKING THE FIRST DAY OF CLASS

———

"There is only one thing that makes a dream impossible to achieve: the fear of failure."

—PAULO COELHO[27]

Before Asenette arrived on Brown's campus she was filled with an ocean of emotions. A wave of relief flushed over her for getting a college acceptance, but most importantly, for finding a college and a community that she could call home. Just as she was settling in, sitting in the green expanse of a local park, feeling the comforting summer sun on her face, another wave came over her, this one not as pleasant. Asenette began to worry about what her life at Brown would be like. Was she prepared for the rigor of a place like Brown?

———

27 Ekaterina Walter, "30 Powerful Quotes on Failure," *Forbes*, January 3, 2018.

Would she fit in there? Was there anything she could do to prepare?

Questions circled her brain endlessly, questions she did not have the answer to. In an attempt to settle her worries she began researching pre-orientation programs. If only she could get to campus a few weeks before anyone else, she was sure she could acclimate to campus life and start her college career on better footing.

After looking through the offerings for summer programs, Asenette decided to apply to a program aimed at helping underrepresented students, many of whom were first-generation and low-income students, prepare for life at Brown. A few short months after applying, Asenette made her way to Brown and began settling in at her home away from home. Through the orientation program, Asenette gained both the academic knowledge and the support system to feel well-equipped to be successful throughout her college career.

Asenette describes the friend group she made at the pre-orientation program stating, "We built a community off of our shared experience... because of that, my experience first year was pretty good since I didn't experience much culture shock coming to Brown." She attributes her participation in the pre-orientation program as one of the most valuable experiences that helped her achieve a smooth transition from high school into college and ensure that she was set up for success at Brown from the start.

The community Asenette made during the program also helped teach her about a concept she hadn't considered before: self-advocacy. Coming from a Latino family, Asenette revealed that self-advocacy wasn't something that was frequently talked about. She elaborates, "We're not really brought up to think it's our right to go to a professor and ask questions."

In an article about self-advocacy, Vivian Nunez echoes a similar sentiment explaining, "In Hispanic culture, there is a common saying: '*Calladita te ves más bonita*,' or 'you look prettier with your mouth shut.'"[28] As a result, it wasn't until Asenette arrived at Brown that she realized asking questions, being an active class participant, and going to office hours wasn't just a student's right, it was an expectation from faculty. It isn't a burden to ask for help. On the contrary, it is a great disadvantage to a student's academic and professional development to not take advantage of the resources available to them.

But how do you actually put self-advocacy into practice?

Dr. Vijay Pendakur has been involved in the diversity and inclusion space for many years. His work and dedication to serving the first-generation, low-income student community has taken him to higher education spaces across the nation. He has held diversity leadership roles at numerous universities and currently serves as the chief diversity officer at a tech company. Dr. Pendakur has also served as an advisor for the National Institutes of Health (NIH) to increase diversity and inclusion initiatives in biomedical career pathways. His roles across a variety of institutions means that Dr. Pendakur

---

28   Vivian Nunez, "Self-Advocacy Is a Learned Skill," *Forbes*, June 17, 2016.

has a well-rounded understanding of the kinds of issues that underrepresented students face in higher education. While he himself was not a FLI student, he understands the resources and support systems that are essential in college spaces to make sure students are successful.

Using Dr. Pendakur's knowledge as a guide, let's walk through what you can expect during your first day of class.

MAKING A CLASSROOM SMALL

Here are some actionable items he highly recommends students do to better navigate the classroom space and build effective relationships with peers and professors.

1. Always Sit in the Front

When you're sitting in the front you're looking right at the professor, and all the noise of the three hundred students behind you will filter out.

2. Introduce Yourself

On the first day of school, get to class ten minutes early and introduce yourself to the faculty member. Walk up and say, "Hi, my name is Vijay, and I'm a first-generation college student. I'm going to be working my way through school, and it's a pleasure to meet you. I'm really looking forward to doing well in your class."

While this may feel uncomfortable at first, know that faculty members will appreciate the extra effort. Being surrounded by faculty members for most of his career, Dr. Pendakur knows that "the vast majority of faculty, even when they're not using the most inclusive practices and the most equity minded practices in their hearts, really want their students to succeed." Going up and introducing yourself to the professor on the first day signals to them that you might be coming back to ask for help during the quarter. That's how faculty members get to know you and become more willing to help you during times of need.

3. Be Absurdly Bold

Now that you've arrived to class early, introduced yourself to the professor, and are sitting at the front waiting for class to begin, look around at the people around you. Introduce yourself to the person sitting to your left and your right. Some good conversation starters include:

- Hi, my name is… What's your name?
- Why are you taking this class?
- What year are you?
- Would you want to study together?

It might be absolutely terrifying to do this on the first day of school because you don't want to stand out. You're probably worried about rejection. What if they think you're weird for talking to them out of nowhere? Dr. Pendakur admits that following these tips is not easy, but once you do them a few times you'll realize that something good always comes out of taking a risk. Chances are one of the people you introduced yourself to will reach out to form a study group when midterms come around, or you can always reach out to them and form your own study group. It's the small steps that add up and help you build a network among peers and faculty members that help ensure you can be academically successful in college.

A SYLLABUS IS YOUR ROADMAP TO CLASS

Social capital is a theory indicating that "students derive benefits like institutional resources, information, and support through their social networks to achieve success in higher education."[29] In other words, it points at how there are actions that certain students learn from their network—parents, faculty, mentors, and so on—that FLI students are not exposed to.

One of the greatest manifestations of social capital is the syllabus. That one sheet of paper that usually ends up misplaced after the first few weeks of the quarter is often underestimated in terms of importance. For those students who have never even heard the word "syllabus" before, that piece of paper passed out on the first day of class is like reading IKEA instructions—confusing as hell. Yet, this confusion is only because students have not yet discovered how much of a hidden treasure map a syllabus really is.

Dr. Pendakur sheds light on the exclusivity of a syllabus when he explains, "If you're a high social capital, multi-generational college goer you know to read a syllabus as the hidden transcript of how to succeed in a class." As a son of a university professor, Dr. Pendakur remembers getting lessons on

---

29 Daniel J. Aleida, et al., "How Relevant Is Grit? The Importance of Social Capital in First-Generation College Students' Academic Success," *Journal of College Student Retention: Research, Theory & Practice* (June 2019).

how to read a syllabus before he even got to high school. His father would sit him down and decipher the code on exactly how to get an A in that class. Now looking back, he sees that as a tremendous social capital transfer that was imperative to his success in high school and college.

The way Dr. Pendakur sees it, syllabi are "actually a blueprint of how to succeed in class, but [professors] don't tell you that." Let's take office hours, for example. A syllabus can state that Professor Smith's office hours are Monday, Wednesday, and Friday from 9 to 11 a.m. But what it doesn't say is what office hours are for or why you should be going to them. After years in the higher education space, Dr. Pendakur has realized that the concept of office hours is an "assumed knowledge that first generation students oftentimes don't have and are intimidated to take advantage of, but multi-generational college goers know this."

In many ways, he sees syllabi as some of the most foundational and canonical elements of the classroom that "actually act as a sorting mechanism for who has privilege and who doesn't." In this way, first-generation college students begin with a disadvantage even before the class actually begins. If students can't understand *how* to be successful in a class, how are they supposed to?

A syllabus can be complex to understand, but let's break it down piece by piece to make sure you know how to read it when you get handed one on the first day of class.

UNDERSTANDING A SYLLABUS

1. Contact Information

What you will always see at the top of the syllabus is the course title, the professor's name, and a teaching assistant's name (if applicable to the course), along with their emails and office hours. This information tells you *who* to contact when you have questions and *how* you can best reach them. More information on what office hours are will be discussed later in this chapter.

2. Textbooks and Course Materials

This section of the syllabus will tell you what things you need for the course, like textbooks, lab notebooks, or workbooks. Note that some materials might be required while others might be recommended, so ask your professor what *is* required to keep your book costs low. It is also worth asking whether your professor is okay with electronic versions of the books since e-versions are usually cheaper.

3. Homework/Lecture Policies

In this section, professors usually explain what the expectations are for turning in homework. Some professors might want you to submit homework online, others might only take homework in person. Same with lecture policies: Some professors may count attendance at lectures as a part of your class grade, others may not take attendance at all. The better you understand what the professor expects of you, the more you can ensure that you are successful in any given class.

4. Course Calendar

The course calendar will include important dates for the class. If you have any field trips or mandatory movie screenings, these dates will all be on the calendar. You will also find exam and midterm dates on it. Make note of all the dates in this section! Missing or forgetting one of these dates can be extremely detrimental to your grade.

5. Grading Rubric

The grading rubric will tell you how your professor is actually grading you. Some professors may include things like participation or lecture attendance. Most commonly you will see things like homework, exams, labs (if you're in a STEM class), or midterms. By understanding a rubric you can figure out exactly what you need to do to get a good grade in the class.

OFFICE HOURS ARE KEY

Office hours are a weekly time a professor or teaching assistant (TA) sets up where they are available to you, the student. Some professors will hold office hours in their physical office space, others might choose a convenient location on campus like a library or a coffee shop. Regardless of where they are, professors expect students to show up, ask questions, and just talk.

Higher income students are more likely to know not only what office hours are, but also how to take advantage of them. Even for students who do know what they are, meeting with a professor one-on-one can seem like an incredibly daunting task, especially for first-generation students. According to Professor Anthony Jack, "The students who are least likely to go to office hours are the students who would benefit from them the most."[30]

The unspoken expectation of office hours is this: *Just go.* Even if you don't have any questions, even if you understand the classroom content fairly proficiently, even if it's only the first day of class, *just go.* Once you start going to office hours regularly you not only get better with classroom material, but you also establish a better relationship with your professors. Once your professors get to know you, they are more likely to connect you to resources, internships, and other academic and professional opportunities. If your professors' office hours conflict with your work schedule, feel free to reach out to them and see if they have other available times for you to meet.

While these might seem like a lot of things to keep track off, take everything one action item at a time.

ACTION CHECKLIST
- ☐ Make a list of questions in the first week of class that you want to ask your professors during office hours. Examples could look like:
  - ☐ What research are they working on? Are there any additional resources they would recommend for the class?
  - ☐ Make sure to introduce yourself to your professors!

---

30 Elissa Nadworny, "College Students: How To Make Office Hours Less Scary," *NPR*, October 5, 2019.

☐ Add professors' office hours into your calendar and treat it like a non-negotiable commitment.

☐ Go through all your syllabi and highlight your professors' email, office hours, office hours location, and important dates in the class.

CHAPTER 6

FINDING THE "YOU" IN COMM-YOU-NITY

———

"Citizenship in any community, however, means more than just being physically present in a certain place. It is about a feeling of belonging in that place, a feeling that shapes your sense of who you are."

—ANTHONY JACK[31]

FEELING OUT OF PLACE

Classroom competition threatens FLI students as it sparks fear that what they perceive to be their intellectual inferiority may be discovered. The more students feel like an imposter on a day-to-day basis, the more they may become disengaged, stop going to class, or even consider dropping out altogether.

———

31 Anthony Abraham Jack, *The Privileged Poor: How Elite Colleges Are Failing Disadvantaged Students* (Cambridge: Harvard University Press, 2020), 182.

On the day of convocation, Gabby remembers standing in front of Rockefeller, the iconic nondenominational church on UChicago's campus. Its massive gothic architecture loomed over her and her fellow first years, welcoming them to a college experience marked by gargoyles and problem sets. On that day Gabby stood in between two housemates waiting as students slowly trickled into Rockefeller and found their seats. She was busy taking in the architecture, the smooth limestone, and the ivy when she first heard the comment.

"Ladies, I got the goose under my bed."

She turned to see a guy from her dorm smiling playfully. Gabby didn't understand. Did this guy actually have a *goose* under his bed? She had heard UChicago was quirky, but a goose as a roommate was certainly pushing the limits. She responded asking, "I'm sorry—you have a goose?"

"A Canada goose!"

A goose from Canada? Gabby still wasn't fully understanding. After asking more clarifying questions she was able to reach the conclusion that the notorious "Canada Goose" was actually a type of winter coat. As she finally found an empty seat in one of the pews, she began to think about this Canada Goose. She needed to buy a winter coat soon too, so maybe she should look into those. The guy did seem incredibly excited by his new winter coat. As soon as convocation was over and she began to make the walk back to her dorm room, she pulled out her phone and googled the winter coat brand. As soon as she got on the website, she nearly had a heart attack: $1,095 for a winter coat? What kind of person was able to afford this?

Her mind tried to make sense of this new discovery. While she considered an $80 coat to be a luxury splurge, her peer was spending almost fourteen times that! What Gabby didn't know was that this was going to be the first of many instances where she would be forced to grapple with the pervasive wealth gap on campus. She would be starting college in a sea of incredibly wealthy and privileged students for whom a $1,095 winter coat was normal.

Surrounded by this prevalent wealth can make it hard not to feel like an imposter. You can feel like you are the only one thinking about how much you can afford to spend on going out, groceries, and social events. At times it can even make you question if you deserve to be on that college campus in the first place. Imposter syndrome is crucial to understand because it can touch all aspects of college life and hinder a student's ability to feel a sense of belonging on their campus.

IMPOSTER SYNDROME

Imposter syndrome is not an unfamiliar sentiment among students of color, especially in predominantly white spaces. However, many studies have found that it is also a common feeling among the first-generation low-income student population. Incredibly competitive classroom environments, for example, "may invoke threat among FG (first generation) students and highlight the fear that their perceived intellectual inferiority may be 'found out.'"[32] I first encountered this feeling of imposter syndrome with my cousin DJ during his first year of college.

My first memory of DJ is seeing him from across the hall of our elementary school. He was standing in line, perfectly behind his classmate. I mirrored his stance, as I stood in line behind a girl in pigtails. Before I could look away, we made eye contact. "*Hi, Diestefano!*" I thought to myself. For many years this was how we communicated—developing an unspoken language of our own. Our moms didn't understand why we didn't actually talk to each other at school, but we didn't mind this secret language at all. From the time I was younger I remember thinking that I wanted to be just like DJ when I grew up; smart, dedicated, and hard-working.

The summer before starting my freshman year at the University of Chicago, I remember DJ inviting me to a get-together with him and other current UChicago students. It was a very sorbet-colored evening as the sun painted pink and orange hues across the sky. With each bite of pizza from Medici's, a frequented restaurant near campus, I heard stories from other Latinx students and how they had managed to find their community in a campus that physically didn't look like their high schools, elementary schools, or hometowns. DJ had remained rather quiet that evening. Then slowly, he began to open up, his story unraveling like a San Marcos blanket.

---

32 Elizabeth A. Canning, et al., "Feeling Like an Imposter: The Effect of Perceived Classroom Competition on the Daily Psychological Experiences of First-Generation College Students," *Social Psychological and Personality Science* (July 2020).

One of the first things DJ mentioned was arriving at UChicago in the fall of 2015 and experiencing imposter syndrome. I was unfamiliar with the term at the time, but DJ would write an article his fourth year of college exploring his experience with imposter syndrome and explaining it as a "pattern of behavior where you will doubt your accomplishments and feel a lack of self-confidence and anxiety."[33] When I read that article for the first time, I couldn't help but feel surprised. DJ had always been the star student in elementary school. Teachers always loved to gush about him and how excited they were to see what his future would hold. What had changed?

Coming from a private, predominantly white high school, DJ felt more than prepared to succeed academically at the University of Chicago. He jokingly described entering college with "as much confidence as Michael Jordan did when he hit the game-winning shot against the Utah Jazz in the 1998 NBA finals."[34] Yet as I sat with him that day, I could tell that even in his first year at UChicago something had changed within him and with his perception of his academic preparedness. If he had felt so prepared going in yet so taken aback and feeling like an imposter when he actually started college, I wondered if I would feel the same. Lost in my thoughts, I scooped Trader Joe's cookie butter ice cream into a small bowl. Nothing like ice cream to get me out of my own head.

---

33   Diestefano Loma, "What Every First-Gen Student Needs to Know about Attending a Predominately White Institution," *Education Post*, May 20, 2019.

34   Ibid.

DJ and I didn't touch the subject of imposter syndrome or attending a predominantly white institution until the end of my fourth year at UChicago. By this point, I had now become well-versed in the struggles of first-generation, low-income students and even had my own moments of self-doubt. DJ had also already secured his first full-time job as an admissions counselor at UChicago. That day we were at a club meeting during a study-break. We were supposed to be taking a break from all things academics, but something about that day had us pick up the conversation that we had dropped off so many years prior. We sat on a windowsill in one of the Harry Potter-esque buildings on campus.

Under the watch of gargoyles and dark wooden beams, DJ began to open up about what the rest of his college career had looked like. He explained that after his freshman year he had continued to struggle academically until being placed on academic probation in the winter quarter of his third year. After this point the imposter syndrome got so bad that it began to inhibit his ability to bounce back. Quarter after quarter, class after class, he began to wonder if he would graduate on time, eventually spiraling into a cycle of anxiety attacks. DJ admitted that "where before [he] simply acted, [he] now began to hesitate." He began to question why he'd even been admitted to such a prestigious university.

In the midst of his difficulties, he leaned on his support system of advisors, friends, and faculty to help him overcome the challenges he was facing. Whether that meant seeking counseling, rearranging his extracurricular commitments, or prioritizing self-care, DJ was willing to do whatever it took to find his footing again. And that he did! Near the end of his senior year he accepted a role as an Admissions Counselor at UChicago to help prepare incoming FLI students for what college life might look like.

DJ opened up to me about the excitement of his new role, saying, "I appreciated the individuals that made a positive impact in my life, and I look to make the road travelled easier for these students than it was for me. I understand how much of a culture shock it is to come into a PWI and navigate the academic and social aspect, but the road to get to college is another mountain to climb in and of itself. Regardless of what college these students apply to or attend, I look to take away that doubt and to ensure students are confident and recognize their potential, so that they always reach for the sky."

As a Spanish speaker, DJ also has the unique opportunity to overcome the language barrier that can exist between prospective families and the college environment. The ability to give back to his community in this way and share his story is what DJ finds most rewarding about his job. He's been able to "help more students from CPS through office hours, give Spanish information sessions, and talk to community-based organizations on how to craft an essay. Hearing from students and their parents on how grateful they are for speaking to them and being available to help at any time drives me to follow my dream."

Whenever speaking with a prospective or incoming student, DJ does not hesitate to share his words of wisdom for navigating the college space. He always makes sure to encourage FLI students that they deserve to be on campus and to seek help when they need it. He reflects on his own experiences, explaining, "Rather than internalizing the conflict and letting it eat you, being able to talk it out does take away a great weight. It helps to deal with the anxiety that comes with having to meet expectations and goals. You don't have to walk alone." He found this camaraderie and sense of community in cultural organizations on campus.

FINDING COMMUNITY, FINDING BELONGING

Coming from a wealthy and predominantly white high school, DJ was familiar with how important it was to find community within that space. Back in high school, the Latinx community had offered him that sense of community and support that was essential for his well-being. As a result, it was finding that same Latinx community that was top of mind as he began his undergraduate career at UChicago. He knew that finding a space and a group of people who he could identify with would help make the high-school-to-college transition much simpler.

On the day of the RSO (Registered Student Organization, UChicago's version of "clubs") fair, DJ felt more than ready to go out and introduce himself to the different Latinx organizations on campus. He walked around the cobblestone steps, carefully eyeing the various tables spread across the main quad. It had rained the day before, so the uneven cobblestones splashed some water on his sneakers as he walked around. After a few minutes he heard salsa music start playing. He stopped for a moment, listening intently to identify what direction the music was coming from. He was standing at the center of the quad at a crossroads. Should he go right, or left?

At last he decided to take a chance and go left. Just a few tables down he could already begin to see students dancing salsa on the sidewalk, backpacks tossed aside. He had found his people. On that day DJ decided to join the two Latinx organizations at UChicago: Movimiento Estudiantil Chicanx de Aztlán (MEChA) and the Organization of Latin American Students (OLAS). In MEChA he found a community of Latinx students exploring the intersections of cultural identity and activism. Meanwhile, in OLAS, he found a more social organization focused on appreciating different Latin American cultures and traditions and keeping them alive.

After four years of being an active member of both communities, he found them to be crucial factors to developing his sense of belonging on campus. DJ admits that both organizations gave him a sense of community and cultural understanding. Whether he was participating in cultural shows, learning new dances, or just finding friends, he loved feeling like he was a part of something bigger than himself and that he had people there to support him when he needed it.

Being a part of MEChA and OLAS and attending their weekly meetings gave DJ a space where he felt comfortable—a safe space of sorts where he was able to be himself and explore parts of his identity beyond that of being a student. With MEChA and OLAS, he found a home away from home with people who could relate to what it meant to be Latino, first-generation, low-income, and a student of color at a predominantly white institution.

EVERYTHING IS GOING TO BE OKAY

As DJ walks around campus now, five years from the date when he first moved in, he can't help but look back and see all the things that he was able to accomplish despite the challenges he faced. Yet, he realizes he was lucky. He had it in himself to seek counseling when he needed it, and he had a supportive network of individuals ready to step up and lend a hand when he needed it. Not all FLI students are that lucky.

Now that he works in the admissions office, he can't help but want to make sure that FLI students who come to campus feel ready to succeed both academically and socially. FLI students are set to face so many challenges that many traditional students won't ever have to overcome. For this reason, it is even more important they feel like they have a community and network to fall back on.

As an admissions counselor, DJ feels like a big part of his job is reassuring students that everything is going to be okay. He never hesitates to share his story and remind students that the FLI student journey is not the conventional student journey. Although DJ had previous experience in predominantly white spaces, college was a different ball game that required learning its own sets of rules and norms. For DJ, this meant that it took him more than the traditional four years to graduate, and that is just fine.

If he could go back and start college over, he would treat himself with more grace and realize that everything is going to be okay. He elaborates saying, "I wasn't really sure what to do first year, whether it was finding an internship or just being proactive. There's a sense of comfort in the sense that you're not going to be the only one who faces these struggles, but in the end that's okay because you'll find a community that's like you and faces similar struggles and you'll be able to work on them together. You're not alone in this process."

Just because your background might feel a whole universe away when compared to the wealthy peers around you, remember that feeling different isn't always bad. Celebrate what got you to where you are and the incredible value that *you* are bringing to your campus.

It might take you a while to find a sense of comfort and community in a new space. Fortunately, this is not a struggle that is unique to one student. This is a struggle that thousands face nationwide. Not only is it a common struggle among FLI students, but it is also an imperative one to address given the detrimental effects that imposter syndrome can have. One study cites, "The more FG (first-generation) students feel like an imposter on a day-to-day basis, the more they may become disengaged, stop going to class, or even consider dropping out of the class altogether—and all of these behaviors may have negative implications for classroom performance."[35]

While in the moment it may feel like you're going through something alone, it is important to remember there are support systems and resources on campus to ensure that you

---

35 Elizabeth A. Canning, et al., "Feeling Like an Imposter: The Effect of Perceived Classroom Competition on the Daily Psychological Experiences of First-Generation College Students," *Social Psychological and Personality Science* (July 2020).

succeed. Some types of organizations you can look for on your campus can include centers for first-generation, low-income students, cultural centers or centers for undocumented or DACA-mented students, centers for students with disabilities, LGBTQIA+ centers, or even your dorm community.

UChicago, for example, has a house system in the dorms, which meant I had two Resident Assistants (RAs) and Resident Heads (RHs)—a family with four kids who lived in the dorm with us—who I could go to for help. Positions like advisors, counselors, RAs, and RHs are there for you, *especially* when times get tough.

College isn't just about getting a diploma; it's about learning about yourself, immersing yourself in a new environment, and taking care of yourself.

ACTION CHECKLIST
☐ Make a list of the identities that are important to you. What organizations and resources on campus align most closely to those identities?
☐ When times get tough, make a list of campus resources you can seek out, including, but not limited to, student health services, student counseling services, and more.

CHAPTER 7

HOW TO DEVELOP PERSONAL RELATIONSHIPS

———

"I think for low-income first-gen students just because they are surrounded by people, often that they have never encountered in their high schools it can be overwhelming to feel like you don't know what you're doing and everybody else does."

—BONNIE KANTER

As a first-year student at UChicago you are bombarded by advice of where to study, what classes to enroll in, and what resources to take advantage of. I remember very early on in my college career I already had one of those messages ingrained in my brain: *Go to the CCSS (Center for College Student Success), because they have free printing and a lending library.* In college terms, the CCSS was the pot of gold at the end of the rainbow, and I was determined to get a share.

Little did I know that the CCSS held an even greater treasure: Bonnie Kanter.

During my first year she was an advisor for FLI students, yet she was known as more than just your typical advisor. Bonnie made students feel heard, understood, and like she was their biggest advocate. She was known across the FLI community as the person to go to when you needed anything, from an advisor signature to someone to vent to. She was always there.

Bonnie first came to UChicago in 2001 for a position in Career Advancement. Not long after that, in 2003, she transitioned into the advising office. It was precisely in this position that she got to see firsthand the challenges that first-generation, low-income students experienced when they moved into UChicago's campus in the fall. In an effort to address some of these issues, she created programming for Chicago Public School (CPS) high school students, priming them for what their college experience might hold. She emphasized programming on areas like moving off campus and studying abroad. Bonnie also had upperclassmen and former CPS graduates to act as mentors for students.

Eventually these programs expanded to other UChicago low-income students. Simultaneously, Bonnie took over College Bridge, a program funded through CPS that allowed students to take classes at UChicago while they were still in high school. UChicago continued the program once CPS cancelled it. When these Bridge students were admitted to UChicago, they would automatically become Bonnie's advisees.

As such, Bonnie became a person who students had a relationship with and felt like they could trust even before they moved to campus in the fall of their freshman year. She was a familiar face in the midst of so much uncertainty. After more than ten years in the advising office, Bonnie shares some of the ways she helped FLI students crack the code to navigate the college scene.

PERSONAL RELATIONSHIPS ARE ESSENTIAL

Many first-generation, low-income students arrive on college campuses "unfamiliar with the new codes and customs of college [and] they struggle to adjust and adapt. The struggle is especially acute for those attending elite institutions." Professor Anthony Jack explains that the lack of a social and academic network FLI students start college with gives them a disadvantage when compared to their higher income peers. As mentioned in previous chapters, one of these "codes and customs" includes building relationships on campus with professors, advisors, and administrators, among others.[36]

This challenge of building relationships is precisely why one of Bonnie's biggest pieces of advice is to focus on them when you first get to college. She especially encourages seeking out mentors in the college space.

A mentor doesn't always have to come through a structured mentorship program at your university. You don't even

---

36 Anthony Abraham Jack, *The Privileged Poor: How Elite Colleges Are Failing Disadvantaged Students* (Cambridge: Harvard University Press, 2020), 19.

have to call this person your mentor if that word makes you uncomfortable. At the very basic sense of the word, a mentor is someone who you can go to for help or advice when you need something. It can be an older student, an administrator, a faculty member, or even an advisor. What matters is that this is someone you feel comfortable asking for advice. You can find your mentor anywhere, from your residence hall, to your sports team, or even your theatre group.

Whenever she's sitting in front of a first-year student, Bonnie pushes them to start finding that mentor figure at UChicago. She highly encourages them to find two types of mentors: a student and a faculty member. She explains her reasoning by stating, "An older student from the [FLI] community could really be an advice giver and an administrator of some kind, whether that be a faculty member or an advisor [who] could try to help [you] develop relationships coming in and make [you] feel comfortable asking for advice."

Bonnie finds these two types of mentorship roles especially important because it creates a space for students to put their confusion and discomfort. She elaborates that while building personal relationships may be hard, it is precisely in these relationships that "students can start to get rid of their doubts and feel like they belong."

You don't have to come in the first day of college ready to build relationships like your life depends on it, but you do have to come in willing to try things that may feel uncomfortable at first. Ease your way into it. See how your classmates do it. Make a game plan. Regardless of what you do, never ever stay quiet. Staying quiet only hurts one person: *you*. Research reaffirms the importance of student engagement, noting "the more actively engaged students are—with college faculty and staff, with other students, and with the subject matter they study—the more likely they are to learn, to stick with their studies, and to attain their academic goals."[37]

HOW TO BUILD RELATIONSHIPS WITH PROFESSORS

After working with students year after year, Bonnie began to realize that one of the biggest obstacles FLI students had to overcome was their discomfort in asking questions. As a FLI student, you're entering a new environment that may be very different from your high school. In college, you'll encounter people who have vastly different backgrounds from you. You have students coming from public schools, private schools, boarding prep schools, and everything in between. For first-generation, low-income students especially, Bonnie admits, "it can be overwhelming to feel like you don't know what you're doing and everybody else does." As the saying goes, you've essentially gone from being a big fish in a small pond to a small fish in a big pond.

What do you do when you feel lost on campus or can't follow what's going on in class? Ask questions! This is, of course, far easier said than done. But there are small steps you can take to ease out of your comfort zone! If you have a question, start by asking your roommate for help. Then, your Resident Assistant (RA), then an advisor, then a faculty member. Slowly

---

37   Kay McClenney, et al., "Student Engagement and Student Outcomes: Key Findings from CCSSE Validation Research," *Community College Survey of Student Engagement* (2007).

build your comfort with asking questions. This is something I personally struggled with a lot. Even coming from a private high school in Chicago's Gold Coast—"gold" because it is one of the richest neighborhoods in the city—I still felt intimidated by all of the smart people around me. Yet, I realized the only way to keep learning was to ask questions.

During my computer science class sophomore year, I was afraid to ask even small clarifying questions in class. Over the course of the quarter, these small clarifying questions grew into larger conceptual questions. The culmination of all of these unanswered questions resulted in large knowledge gaps I had with the class material. And now with an entire quarter's worth of information that I didn't understand, I was forced to ask my professor to sit down and help me. She was clearly disappointed I had not come to her earlier.

After this experience I decided it was worth the risk of asking "dumb" questions in class. I asked professors to clarify a point they made in class. I asked my peers to explain things again if we were studying together. What I learned after taking the risk and asking questions is, more often than not, there is someone else in the room who will share that same question with you. As a result, no question is a dumb one, because it is helping both you and someone else learn more.

HOW TO ASK QUESTIONS AT OFFICE HOURS

One of the places to practice asking questions is at office hours. From Bonnie's years in academic advising and in the higher education space, she has observed that "the successful students at college campuses are often the ones who spent time getting to know faculty, [yet] that is an incredibly intimidating prospect for many low-income first-generation students."

To be completely honest, I also felt intimidated back when I started college. Many of my close friends would go to office hours the first week just to get to know the professor. Although I never vocalized this, one of my biggest questions about going to office hours was *how*? How could I make sure that I didn't ask a "dumb" question and felt confident walking into office hours? I knew I wanted to be that girl who walked in, hair blowing in the wind, textbook in hand, asking those enquiries that made the professor say, "Wow, I hadn't considered that before. Great question!"

As I did with all my questions during my first two years of college, I knocked on Bonnie's door, urging her to shower me with her wisdom. Bonnie shared the story of a previous low-income student who, like me, had been nervous to even think about office hours. How did she conquer her fear? She would walk into office hours, head held high and confident. When the professor was available she would take out the book they were reading in class, and then—and here comes the secret—she would randomly pick a paragraph and ask the professor to walk her through that part of the text.

Yes, I know this sounds simple. Maybe so simple that you don't think it will work. But from my experience and Bonnie's, professors love to talk about the material they are going over in class. Asking about an excerpt of a book or a chapter is a great way to get a conversation started with a professor and begin feeling more comfortable in that space. It's also worth noting that going to office hours isn't just about asking questions. It's about building relationships with professors.

Faculty and professors want to get to know you, and they can be invaluable resources throughout your academic career and beyond. When speaking to your professors, don't be afraid to open yourself up and really be genuine about where your interests lie and how they can help you succeed. Ready to take a chance and walk into office hours for the first time? Here are some quick tips before stepping into your professors' office:

1. Questions don't necessarily have to be about material you don't understand. Some other topics you can ask questions about include:
    a. Their research projects and research interests;
    b. Elaborating on class material;
    c. Recommended readings outside of the syllabus;
    d. Recommendations for internships or jobs or their experience in a particular career path; or
    e. Recommendations on similar courses offered on your campus if you really like their course.
2. Write down questions during class and as you read through the material. Bring these questions to office hours and ask them there!

Have a few questions prepared for your professor now? Head on in! You'll be surprised by how far the conversation and the relationship will take you.

MAKING PROFESSORS YOUR ALLIES

During the beginning of her college career, Sandra Busta-mante didn't understand how students were supposed to use their professors as resources. It wasn't until she began talking to some of her classmates that she realized office hours might actually be a helpful resource for her. Sandra decided to give them a shot herself and go. While office hours were certainly helpful in working through homework assignments and getting further clarification on class material, she realized there was an unspoken benefit to establishing relationships with professors.

After becoming a regular at office hours, her professor began recommending various conferences and programs she thought might be a great fit for Sandra. Not wanting to say no to any opportunity, Sandra applied to all kinds of programs and was able to do a variety of academic and professionally enriching activities, including a Public Policy hackathon—a place where numerous students come together to collaborate and engage on a particular issue—at Carnegie Mellon University's Heinz School of Public Policy. It was in doing these various activities that she finally realized how important it was to reach out to professors.

Now Sandra loves to share her story, explaining how "making my professors my biggest allies was so key for me in not only wanting more, but finding more opportunities to make myself better." She pushes college freshmen to make profes-sors their allies, particularly those in their major department. Sandra tells them that relationships with faculty can be the most influential in students finding different resources and opportunities to help them grow and navigate their campus.

While it may feel like a big risk to take that first step and go to office hours, it is definitely a risk worth taking and one that has the possibility to influence the rest of your college career.

HOW TO BUILD RELATIONSHIPS

As a current junior at the University of Texas in San Antonio, Sandra finally feels fluent in the world of building professional relationships. She now leverages the relationships she has built at internships and jobs to help her in landing a job in the public sector. Now that Sandra's younger sister is getting ready to start college, she sits down with her frequently to pass along some advice. In particular, Sandra encourages her sister to seek out at least two different types of organizations: social and professional.

1. Social

For Sandra, social organizations can be anything from joining Greek life, a cultural-based organization, or a religious organization. Find organizations with values and experiences similar to your own. For Sandra, it doesn't matter so much the *type* of organization. What really matters is building a community on campus. She admits that joining campus life organizations are the "key to finding your peers, and especially overcoming that imposter syndrome."

2. Professional

From Sandra's own experience, professional and career organizations are imperative to any student's development in college, especially for first-generation, low-income students. Due to her interest in local government, Sandra decided to join the Texas City Managers Association as a student member.

This program has not only given her two city managers as mentors, but also helped connect her to various job opportunities that might be available to her in the public sector.

Sandra described her relationship with her mentors, stating, "They have been so helpful with advice for college and helping me figure out what I really like. They've shared so much about their job and what their day-to-day functions are and how they got there. They've also been helpful guiding me and telling me, 'This is what you should do if you're still interested in pursuing this path.'" Joining professional networks has helped Sandra gain insight into what it means to work in local government—a valuable experience to have before even working in the field.

While you may not always find a "Bonnie" immediately upon arriving at campus, it's important to make sure you start college open to building relationships with the people around you. As a first year you'll have a plethora of opportunities to meet new people, both faculty and peers alike. When you do, be sure to follow up with people who peak your interest and share either an interest or background with you. Before you know it, you'll slowly start building your support system at your new home away from home.

ACTION CHECKLIST

☐ Prepare questions before class and office hours.

    ☐ Before every class write down questions that you can ask during class. No matter how small you think the question might be, challenge yourself to ask at least one question every class period.

☐ Have a list of questions prepared before you head into office hours. Questions can either be about class material, research interests, or your professors' career.

☐ As you get to know your professors, keep track of what industries they've worked in and how they might be able to help you outside of the classroom.

☐ Identify at least two organizations (one professional, one social) that you want to engage with on your campus and start going to their meetings.

PART 3

JUNIOR YEAR

CHAPTER 8

STRIKING A BALANCE

—

"Poverty has conditioned me to value the things I was given and not ask for more. I realize now I will only stay behind if I simply settle for what I have. I am still trying to learn to seek and ask for more, not because I am greedy, but because by asking for more I will be able to get the adequate resources and opportunities that will allow me to succeed in the environment that I currently exist in."

—GUILLERMO CAMARILLO[38]

I first heard the name Guillermo Camarillo four years ago when a post appeared on my Facebook feed. It was a letter beginning with the words, "So I went to the dentist today. And wrote an open letter of my experience: Dear Dentist..." At first, I wasn't sure what to make of the letter. Why would someone write a letter to their dentist and post it on social media? As I continued to read, I understood. When Guillermo disclosed to his dentist that he couldn't get braces

---

38 Guillermo Camarillo, "Why Poor College Kids Like Us Need to Start Asking for the Help We Need," *Education Post*, May 13, 2017.

because he was moving to Palo Alto to attend Stanford in the fall, his dentist responded in complete disbelief.

In his letter Guillermo describes,

You immediately jumped to ask me what my ACT score was? It was weird cause I have never had a professional ask me that. I answered honestly. Your response after that clearly showed what you were thinking.

You sarcastically said, "Wow you got (blank) on the ACT?! And you got into Stanford?"

I was confused. I had always thought my ACT score wasn't too bad...

You then said, "Well, my daughter got a 35 and she didn't get into Stanford. She goes to UMich."

But you didn't stop there, you kept going.

You said, "Well, when you have kids from neighborhoods like THESE, like you know, ENGLEWOOD. It's easy for them to get into Harvard or Stanford with a (states my score)."

You kept going. You said, "You know, when kids go to schools around here (AKA public schools in minority neighborhoods), it's easier for them to get into schools like Stanford. My daughter goes to a school where like 20 kids get perfect ACT scores."

I stayed quiet.

He continued, "You're very lucky. Consider yourself very lucky. Getting into Stanford is like competing on The Voice, you know, when you get the buzzer."[39]

In his letter, Guillermo reflects on his dentist's complete disbelief that a student like him could get into a school like Stanford. Guillermo utilized his post to shed light on being underestimated as a Latino student coming from a low-income community in Chicago. According to data from the US Department of Education, in 2016 Hispanic students made up 19.8 percent of enrolled undergraduate students, compared to 52 percent of enrolled white students.[40] Since seeing this post for the first time in 2016, Guillermo Camarillo was a name that popped up multiple times throughout my college years.

After posting his letter, that to this day has over sixty thousand likes and fourteen thousand shares, Guillermo has worked as a Jopwell U Ambassador, helping connect Latinx, Indigenous, and Black students to a variety of career and professional opportunities. In 2018, Guillermo also founded Chicago Latinx Scholars, a virtual community organization focusing on "connecting Latinx high school/college students in the Chicagoland area to opportunities [...] [including] scholarships, internships, jobs, and resources in general."[41] Through these various initiatives, Guillermo has helped foster a community among first-generation, low-income students and professionals in the Chicagoland area, all the while he

---

39   Guillermo Camarillo, *Facebook,* July 18, 2016.

40   Lorelle L Espinosa, et al., "Race and Ethnicity in Higher Education: A Status," *The American Council on Education* (2019).

41   Chicago Latinx Scholars, *Facebook,* December 21, 2016.

was navigating what it meant for him to be a FLI student at Stanford.

HIGH-SCHOOL-TO-COLLEGE TRANSITION

Guillermo grew up in Little Village, a predominantly Mexican/Mexican-American neighborhood on Chicago's West Side. As he was growing up, he was very fortunate to be surrounded by counselors and mentors who encouraged him to push past his inclination to go to a neighborhood high school.

Instead, they motivated him to go to George Westinghouse College Prep, a high school all the way across town with more resources than his neighborhood high school would have been able to offer. Westinghouse was not only named the twenty-eighth best high school in Illinois by *U.S. News & World Report* and the ninth best high school in the city by *Chicago Magazine*, but in 2020 it had the highest five-year graduation rate of any high school in Chicago.[42] Yet, in order to take advantage of these resources and opportunities, Guillermo had to take the train on an hour-long commute to school every day.

Similar to elementary school, his high school experience was full of people supporting his academic journey and encouraging him to apply to selective colleges and universities. Once college acceptance season rolled around, Guillermo decided on Stanford as his new home.

---

42 Leushel Kerry, "George Westinghouse College Prep 2019–2020 School Profile," *George Westinghouse College Prep* (2020).

Hilda Posada, Guillermo's mother, remembers his college acceptance and how proud she and her husband were of their son. She explained how "neither his father or I went to college but we have always given our children everything we can. Even so, we never imagined that our son was going to get so far. Since kindergarten, Guillermo cared about his academics, but I just didn't imagine how far that would take him because us, as undocumented immigrants, we don't ambition for much, just to work hard to be able to survive."[43]

In both high school and elementary school, Guillermo was used to being the straight-A student. A few weeks into his first quarter at Stanford he realized he was not performing as well academically as he had in high school. This realization, compounded by family stressors as his father faced deportation back in Chicago, made his high-school-to-college transition all the more difficult.

As Guillermo tried to acclimate to his life at Stanford while balancing his family situations, he began to ask himself one question over and over again: "I have all this privilege… what am I gonna do with it?" As this question tumbled in his head, he couldn't help but feel guilty. At Stanford he was immersed in privilege and was surrounded by opportunities and resources he could have never dreamed of. Yet in the midst of that comfort, however, his family back in Chicago was struggling.

---

43 Laura Rodriguez, "Against All Odds, Son of Undocumented Parents Goes from Little Village to Stanford University," *The Chicago Tribune*, February 5, 2016.

Having to make sense of both of these realities became increasingly isolating. At Stanford he was surrounded by students who "[could not] fathom the thought that [he] came from the West Side of Chicago or [that] he grew up poor most of his life." Where most college students around him were concerned about getting the perfect internship, Guillermo was worried about how to help his parents pay for next month's rent. This isn't particularly surprising given that for many FLI students, financial hardships are at the forefront of their experience. According to a study from the American Council on Education, "70 percent of Latino undergraduates in higher education come from families in the bottom half of earners."[44]

LEARNING TO BALANCE FAMILY AND ACADEMICS

Growing up, family was always important to Guillermo. When he went off to California to attend Stanford, he found himself having to juggle his academic life and maintaining a relationship with his family from across the country. Guillermo acknowledges that while it's an inherent part of the Latino culture to be very family-oriented, there were times when it was hard to fulfill this expectation. At the beginning of his college career, Guillermo remembers feeling like he had to call home every day to check in on his family. He also admits some part of him didn't want to call home for fear of finding out what challenges were arising back in Chicago.

---

44 Christ Quintana, "More Latino Students than Ever Are Trying to Get Their Degree, but It's Fraught and Costly," *USA Today*, May 24, 2020.

Eventually, he was forced to take a step back and recalibrate his situation. Guillermo decided to take some time from calling home and instead channel his attention toward acclimating to life at Stanford. Guillermo remembers breaking this news to his mom over the phone, telling her, "I'm not gonna call you in some time because I just need a break. I need to breathe and focus on what's going on right now, because this is important and I need to just focus on this."

At first his parents weren't all that understanding of him needing to take some time from calling home, but they eventually came around to his growing need for space. As his Stanford career continued, Guillermo felt like he could open up to his parents about what it meant to be a FLI student. He remembers explaining to them that, while getting into Stanford was an incredible accomplishment, "there [were] a lot of sad and painful moments that [he was experiencing there, such as] times when [he had] to stay up until 5 a.m. doing work because he didn't understand [the material]." His parents eventually realized that going to Stanford required Guillermo's full time and attention.

By disconnecting from home, Guillermo felt like he was able to find an outlet in other extracurriculars on campus. He found comfort in his friend group because they were people who shared a similar background. Guillermo felt like they could relate to him in terms of the personal, family, and financial struggles he was facing. In that sense, he found a community that allowed him to feel more at home on campus and experience that feeling of belonging.

REMAINING TRUE TO YOURSELF

As Guillermo navigated internships and his first job, he had one priority in mind: *Remain true to myself.* He knew as a soon-to-be Stanford graduate, he would have many opportunities available to him. During his search, he wanted to make sure he was choosing a job he genuinely enjoyed. He wanted to be interested in it. He didn't want to just accept the first offer he got.

Throughout his job search, Guillermo realized he had to shift away from taking a family-centric approach and choosing a job that offered him a good salary. If he did this, he knew it would be a "disservice to [himself] because [he] wouldn't be choosing a job that [he] enjoyed. [Instead he] would be choosing it out of necessity to help his family." Consequently, it became his goal to find a job that could help open doors for him in the professional world *and* compensate him well.

It is no secret that college seniors are consistently given advice from peers and mentors. Guillermo remembers getting both solicited and unsolicited insight into various industries and job roles. He had to learn to center himself and think about what was important to *him* and what he could see himself doing after graduation.

Guillermo considered factors like location, compensation, support systems at work, and benefits. One unexpected perk he gained throughout the process was learning to hold transparent conversations with friends about salaries. He explains, "If you're first gen [and] a person of color, you have to have that transparency because you don't know whether or not you're getting underpaid." This was a particularly salient finding for Guillermo because he realized that for many FLI students, the benchmark for looking at compensation packages is their families' income. Given that the median salary of low-income families is $25,624 and college graduates make an average of $50,000, this benchmark puts FLI students at an overwhelming disadvantage.[45] [46]

BE OPEN TO CHANGE

Maddy Molina is a Chicago native and a current undergraduate student at Washington University in St. Louis. While her and Guillermo's stories have some significant differences, Maddy also struggled with finding herself and acclimating to the college environment. After graduating from a private high school on Chicago's North Side, Maddy felt prepared to conquer whatever college threw her way. She had taken prep classes in high school and even participated in a pre-orientation program at Washington University in St. Louis for additional college readiness. While Maddy felt academically ready for the rigor of WashU, she started college thinking she had to be the same person she was in high school.

In a predominantly white high school, Maddy felt the constant pressure to do what was expected of her socially. Whether that meant taking daily Starbuck's runs before school or buying new outfits for every school dance, Maddy

---

45   Elkins, Kathleen, "29 Percent of Americans Are Considered 'Lower Class'—Here's How Much Money They Earn," *CNBC*, September 30, 2019.

46   Abigail Johnson Hess, "College Grads Expect to Earn $60,000 in Their First Job—Here's How Much They Actually Make," *CNBC*, February 20, 2019.

felt like she had to put in a constant effort to fit in to the social scene. She went into WashU thinking the social environment would be similar. A few weeks into her freshman year, though, she began looking to join organizations that she hadn't been able to participate in during high school. At WashU, she got involved in sexual assault prevention clubs and a sorority, among other campus organizations.

While participating in these organizations, Maddy came to the realization that "in high school I very much wanted to be a people pleaser and just morph into whatever they wanted me to be. WashU is similar to my high school in its makeup, but because it's bigger, you can really just find who you want to hang out with. It's a lot easier to not have to morph into someone you're not going to like."

For Maddy, college gave her the time to explore the interests, passions, and ideas she didn't feel like she had the space to do in high school. As a result, she's been able to find the people at WashU whom she shares those same interests with and form closer friendships and relationships. She encourages incoming students to approach college with an open mind and "be open to yourself changing, because I didn't really know I could do that."

LEARNING TO RECALIBRATE

Whether it be in regard to friendships, family relationships, or your relationship with yourself, the first few months (if not years) of college require you to recalibrate. The way you acted in relationships in high school may not necessarily be your preferred method of acting anymore. Your relationship with your family may evolve, whether you decide to move across the country or only a thirty-minute drive away. Entering the world of higher education is a big transition, especially for low-income, first-generation students. For this reason, give yourself the time and the space to acknowledge the changes that come your way and to recalibrate accordingly.

ACTION CHECK LIST

- ☐ Going into college, make a list of the relationships that are important to you (including your relationship with yourself) and how you want to show up for those relationships.
  - ☐ Be sure to communicate your needs and your expectations with the people who are important to you (friends, family, roommates, and others).
- ☐ Revisit that list at least twice a quarter or semester and ask yourself:
  - ☐ Are there any changes that need to be made?
  - ☐ Are these relationships serving me in a positive manner?
  - ☐ Am I showing up for myself and for others in a way that feels good?

CHAPTER 9

NETWORKING AND HOW TO START

"I'm not going to cut your wings. I'm going to let you fly."

—SANDRA, XIOMARA CONTRERA'S MOM

Through a series of fortunate events, I started forming my FLI community much earlier than my first year of college or even first year of high school. Per my mom's request, I joined an enrichment program the summer after sixth grade called High Jump. High Jump is a program that provides "access to education for Chicago middle school students who have exhibited academic ambition and potential and who are of limited economic means."[47]

In more concrete terms, High Jump meant that on Saturdays during the school year and for five weeks during the summer I was taking classes with other low-income students

---

47   High Jump, "High Jump Mission," *High Jump*, 2021.

from across the Chicago area. High Jump was the first time I was surrounded with students who were both incredibly motivated academically and had a similar socioeconomic background as me. High Jump gave me a community of students, teaching assistants, teachers, faculty, and alumni who were engaged in my academic journey and invested in my success. Although she was a few cohorts above me, one of the people I always heard about in the High Jump community was Xiomara Contreras.

Xiomara earned her undergraduate degree from Northwestern University with a major in Communication Studies and a minor in Latina/o Studies. She currently holds the role of Product Marketing Manager at Google. Regardless of where her work and professional life take her, Xiomara remains committed to giving back to the communities that have helped her along her academic and professional journey. While I never got to know Xiomara personally in High Jump, I was surprised by how much of myself I could identify in her experiences as a first-generation Latina growing up in Chicago. I hope you are also able to find a bit of yourself in her story.

PROFESSIONAL EXPECTATIONS IN HIGHER EDUCATION
When Xiomara thinks back to high school, one of the things she loved the most was the genuine love of learning and pursuit of curiosity. Students were pulled by their passions to take classes in subjects they were interested in and even to pursue independent studies. It was a culture of continuous learning for the sake of learning. When she started

at Northwestern, she faced a culture shock in the learning environment.

At Northwestern it seemed like everyone was taking classes for the sake of choosing a major that would end in the highest paying internship or job. Every class became a stepping stone in a broader career journey. A major in economics and communication, for example, became the perfect combination if you wanted to graduate and become a consultant at Deloitte. This culture extended beyond academics and into the world of extracurriculars. During undergrad Xiomara felt like she "had to be in a million clubs [and barely sleep] to feel like a successful Northwestern student."

Post-grad she was also faced with the expectations of finding a job and, more specifically, a high-paying one. College students who already come from families with high paying jobs are fueled by their need to maintain a lifestyle. On the other hand, the urgency for FLI students to find jobs after undergrad is fueled by social mobility, a need to take care of their families, and feeling financially secure.

While Xiomara found those expectations to be incredibly off putting, she could relate to some of them. She knew that as a first-generation college student, she needed to get a job when she graduated. Not having a job was not an option. As much as she hated to admit it, she herself had some metric of success. She wanted to graduate and get a job that could give her health insurance and pay her well. In an effort to meet this metric, Xiomara reminded herself that she "couldn't have invested all this time at Northwestern and sacrificed [her] wellbeing to not get a job." Getting a job was a bare minimum for all the sacrifices she had had to make in college.

PLANTING THE NETWORKING SEED

Upperclassmen are 100 percent your best friends. At least that's how Xiomara felt coming into Northwestern. She remembers coming to Northwestern as a prospective student and meeting many upperclassmen who didn't hesitate in sharing resources, support centers, and advice. Although she hadn't even committed to the school yet she already felt like she had the beginning of a support system, which made her all the more excited to accept a position with the incoming class.

While the leaves on the trees had changed color by the time she moved in during the fall, the upperclassmen were still there, waiting for her on campus. As she began to find her way around campus and classes, it was refreshing to know she already had a group of upperclassmen there to support her through her journey. They helped point her to the spaces on campus where "people of color hang out [and] do their homework," as well as where resources like free printing and events took place.

Unknowingly just hanging out in these spaces meant that she got to hear about resources other students of color were taking advantage of and how she too could get involved with them. That's eventually how she ended up participating in various programs and internships at Northwestern—it was all through word of mouth and with the help of the welcoming upperclassman community.

THE NETWORKING BUD

Networking is a term that is tossed around in the professional and academic community. Students are encouraged to begin building and maintaining their network in high school. Networking is oftentimes at the center of finding professional opportunities and continuing your career growth. A great majority of jobs—80 percent, according to one study—are never advertised, and instead are filled by word of mouth. As a result, "it's who you know and who knows you that matters. You must develop relationships and connections within your network to have more opportunities to advance your career."[48]

When it came time for Xiomara to choose a major, she wasn't sure where to even begin. There were so many options on the major catalogue, many of which sounded interesting. How was she supposed to decide on one? And what career options existed for each of the majors? She knew she really cared about education and social justice. She could see herself working in the nonprofit space one day, but what major aligned with that?

After talking through her interests with one of her upperclassmen "mentors," they suggested she major in Communication Studies. They also suggested she join a program, Management Leadership for Tomorrow (MLT), that was supposed to help her with career prep and make sure she was on the path to graduate with a job offer in hand. In MLT, she learned interview skills, timelines she needed to consider

---

48 American Association of Medical Dosimetrists, "Why Networking Is Important," 2021.

for applying to full-time jobs, and professional development skills. MLT helped give her a framework as to how she should start looking at internships and job offers.

A coach from MLT was ultimately the person who recommended she apply for Google's BOLD internship. Xiomara had never considered an internship at Google before, but she decided to give it a shot. And from there everything changed. She landed the internship position, spending the entire summer learning what it meant to work in a corporate space. She was pleasantly surprised.

Unlike working in finance, banking, or consulting, she felt like the tech culture was a lot warmer and more welcoming. Ultimately, the BOLD internship turned into a full-time job offer before Xiomara even started her senior year of college. Mission accomplished.

While many advisors and professionals are quick to express the importance of having a network, very few sit students down to explain what a network is and how to take advantage of one. For first-generation, low-income students the struggle is even greater. Their family and friends seldom have networks they can already tap into. Instead, they are forced to start from scratch. While Xiomara seemed to get the hang of networking quickly, I, on the other hand, struggled in picking apart the hidden curriculum of networking.

HOW TO FLOURISH AT NETWORKING

N-E-T-WO-R-K. Net-work. Network. Maybe if I said it enough I'd get more comfortable with it. Maybe it's an acquired taste. Maybe I had to let it sit on the tip of my tongue, finding its true flavor. For the Career Advancement woman standing in front of us, it rolled off the tongue. You could tell she was so comfortable networking that she could probably "network" in her sleep. But how exactly could *I* network? Did I even have a network yet? It was only my winter quarter of my freshman year of college, so I hadn't even thought about building professional connections.

To be honest, I was only at this networking event because it was mandatory for my scholarship program. And now I had to have lunch with actual adults, have career conversations, and stay connected? As a fairly introverted college student, this seemed like a nightmare! Suddenly, the cold Chicago weather seemed like a much better place to be. Would anyone notice if I snuck out? Just as I was contemplating the thought, the flow of students pushed me into the dining space. There was no getting out now. I scanned the room looking for anyone I knew. My heart sank when I didn't see anyone I immediately recognized. This was going to be the longest lunch ever.

I sat down at a table that didn't have any people, hoping not too many would show up. Boy, was I wrong. Apparently, it wasn't just the woman who liked to network—all the students around me did too. They walked around in their business casual attire, portfolio full of résumés in hand. They threw out words like *consulting, LinkedIn,* and even asked for business cards. While I was also dressed in business professional attire, I couldn't help but still feel like an imposter. There was a whole new world going on in front of me, one that I didn't fully understand, but could tell was important. I didn't know how just yet, but I knew I was going to have to crack the networking code if I ever wanted to catch up to my fellow UChicago students.

If you find yourself in this position, know you aren't alone. While many college students across the country may seem to have everything figured out, many others—particularly first-generation, low-income students—are left to be wallflowers at these events, losing out on opportunities purely because they've never been in a situation like this before. Luckily, there are some things to keep in mind the next time you find yourself at a networking event like this one.

STEP 1: BUILD YOUR NETWORK

The first step in my quest to build a network began with making a list of any organizations I had been a part of in middle school and high school. For me that meant High Jump, an enrichment program I did as a seventh and eighth grader; Daniel Murphy Scholarship Fund, a scholarship program I was a part of in high school; Cherubs, a theatre conservatory-style summer institute I participated in; and CAAP, a program for first-generation, low-income students at UChicago that I was involved in. Then, I made a list of all the people I felt like I could reach out to at these programs today. I wrote down the names of faculty members, teaching assistants, executive directors, RAs, and others, along with their contact information. Step 1, check.

STEP 2: STAY IN TOUCH

One of the things I was consistently told, even during my first year in college, was to stay in touch. The advice I was usually given was to update my network about the various activities, programs, and internships I was doing to keep them in the loop of my professional and academic journey. At that point in my life I was not completely comfortable doing this. I honestly didn't really think my network would want to know these things and, to be quite honest, doing this felt incredibly awkward (more on this later).

Instead, my way of keeping in touch involved being an active member of the communities and organizations I was a part of. That meant showing up to High Jump Alumni events and helping at fundraisers. It meant staying involved with CAAP and becoming an active member of the FLI community on campus. To me, staying in touch also meant giving back and showing up.

Most of these events took no more than a few hours a month, yet their impact was huge! Showing up meant that the higher ups in these organizations got to know me by name, and as our relationship grew over time they would tell me about programs and opportunities I hadn't known about before. Something I didn't realize back on that cold Chicago winter day was that just by showing up and being active I would be on people's radar, and that's one of the most powerful tools you can utilize.

I recognize that sometimes talking to people, regardless of whether or not they're strangers, can be hard. I remember heading into a networking event once and standing in front of the elevator afraid to head into the room where everyone was gathered. I didn't really know anyone there, and I was afraid of not fitting in. That day in front of the elevator, I told myself that I only had to talk to one person and I could leave after an hour. As soon as I entered the room, I made my way to the food table and struck up a conversation with the person next to me grabbing some fruit. "Hi, I'm Jess. What's your name?" He very kindly responded, and we ended up having a twenty-minute conversation over sparkling water and fruit.

When you don't know what to do, introduce yourself to one person, ask what they do, and follow up about why they decided to go to the event. You'd be surprised by how many people are willing to share their career path, even to strangers.

STEP 3: REACH OUT

In the summer of 2017, I was doing an internship for a non-governmental organization (NGO) in Quetzaltenango, Guatemala. While there, I got the chance to work with two UChicago students and three UChicago Alumni on promoting mealworm consumption as an alternative source of protein for low-income Guatemalan families. During one of my phone calls to my boyfriend at the time, he told me about a talk he had attended given by a doctor at the University of Chicago Medical Center. This doctor, who we will refer to as Doctor X, was doing research on health disparities among Latino populations in Chicago.

Automatically, I was incredibly intrigued by her work and wanted to learn more. I asked if he had gotten any contact information at the conference, and he graciously passed along her email. I knew I wanted to reach out to her, but I didn't feel comfortable with cold emailing. *Would she even respond?* Unsure if I would even send the email, I decided to at least get something written down. It went something like this;

Good Evening Doctor X,
I just arrived back to Chicago a few days ago after spending the summer working in Guatemala. I was wondering if there is a time before the academic year begins in which I could discuss your past and current research with you? After the work I did this summer, I am greatly interested in the work you have been doing and would love an opportunity to learn more about it. Thank you for your time, and I look forward to hearing from you soon.
Jessica Mora

Now looking back, there are so many things I would change. I would be more specific about what interests me about her research. I would tell her a little bit about what I was doing in Guatemala, and I would bring up that I am interested in a research assistant opportunity. However, the above email got the job done. I hit send, and a few days later I got an appointment with Doctor X to talk about her research and eventually ended up getting a research assistant job that I kept for two years. It goes to show that even when you think your chances of a reply are slim, reach out anyway! You never know what might come from it.

STEP 4: BE KIND

Like I mentioned in the previous step, I interned in Guatemala with two other UChicago students. One was a rising senior and one was a rising sophomore like me. We not only worked together but outside of work hours we also explored Quetzaltenango, the second largest city in Guatemala. We went grocery shopping, helped each other out when one of us got sick, and met up at a quaint coffee shop for dessert on an almost daily basis. We even took a weekend vacation together to explore the city of Antigua. It was a great summer to say the least.

When we got back to campus that fall, we made sure to catch up at least once a quarter. We became a dynamic trio where even if we had different majors and prospective career paths, we helped each other out where we could.

By the fall of 2018 when my research assistant job was in danger due to budget cuts, one of the people I had interned with in Guatemala, who I considered a close friend, reached out to me. After graduating in the spring he had gotten a job as a research coordinator at the UChicago Medical Center. He needed research assistants who he trusted and thought our other friend from Guatemala and I would be the perfect women for the job. I worked for him for almost two years, during which he gave me academic advice, career advice, and served as a professional reference when I needed one.

Even when I was contemplating job offers post-grad, he was there to help talk me through my options. This takes me to Step 4: Be kind to those around you. You never know when someone you met once, went to school with, or were in class with is going to be in a position to help you out. You want to be the person they think of when they're hiring or someone asks them for a recommendation. Had I not been a reliable and trustworthy coworker or a good friend, my coworker wouldn't have thought about me when he needed people for the job. My position at the time would have been cut, and I would not have had a job for the rest of the academic year.

STEP 5: COFFEE DATES

After two health-related internships in Latin America during consecutive summers, I went rogue. I took a job with an investment management company in Los Angeles. While I was initially nervous to work in a corporate setting, this internship taught me more about networking than I could have ever imagined. During the week of orientation they sat us down to explain the expectations of the program:

1. Ask questions. Always.
2. Have coffee chats.
3. Feedback. Feedback. Feedback.

The first item seemed pretty straight forward. I could ask questions—no biggie. Although to be honest, asking questions in a corporate setting felt like a whole different ball game. My advice? Make a cheat sheet! If you know you're going to meet someone new or go to a presentation, write questions down beforehand so you have them ready to go when it comes time for Q&A.

Expectation three also seemed relatively understandable. Be receptive to feedback from those who give it, whether it's coming from your supervisor, a fellow intern, or a coworker. Even if you don't agree 100 percent, listen to what they have to say and keep it in mind for the future.

For me, the hardest of the three items was the second one. I was supposed to cold-email various people at the company, both mid- and upper-level management, and ask for a coffee chat to talk about the company, their job, and anything else I wanted to ask them. This was absolutely nerve-wracking! Even two years after the Doctor X email, I still hated cold-emailing. And I especially hated sitting down and talking to strangers.

While I loved getting to hear personal stories about how people found their careers, I hated how formal some of the conversations got. There were times when I was sitting down waiting for my coffee date, palms sweaty, and they would come in, sit down, and bluntly ask, "So what do you want to know?" Whenever this happened my heart would race like I was coming down a roller coaster at full speed. I would start second-guessing myself, wondering if my questions were "good enough." Just thinking about talking to strangers definitely kicked my anxiety into full gear.

In spite of my resistance, I decided to give it a shot. I went ahead and found some interesting people to talk to via the company directory. I began by looking for people I had something in common with. I searched for "University of Chicago," "Latinx," "Nonprofit," and "Education." Then began the cold-emailing process. Writing the email wasn't terrible since all I had to do was follow the email format structure that we had been given as interns. The true test came when people started agreeing to talk to me.

I was so nervous, like singing-in-front-of-your-classmates nervous. While everyone I met up with was incredibly kind, some people were definitely better at easing my nerves than others. There were people who the second we sat down were blunt and less engaged with small talk, which was, as you can imagine, an incredibly intimidating experience and one that felt too formal for my liking.

On the other hand there were people who actually *offered* to take me out for coffee, and we spent more than our allotted time talking about our upbringing and what it meant to be a person of color in a corporate environment. The latter were definitely more up my alley, because they felt more conversational and less professional. However, looking back I'm happy to have gotten both of these kinds of coffee dates, because I know to always prepare for both. I always write down additional questions in case the person I'm meeting with is the more-to-the-point type.

The first few coffee dates felt like I was learning how to swim by being thrown into the deep end of the pool. Yet coffee date after coffee date, I began to slowly learn how not to drown, then how to float, and eventually how to swim. And truthfully, this was one of the most helpful soft skills I have ever learned. Getting to know so many strangers in one summer was the perfect way to become more comfortable in reaching out to people I don't know and speaking up in any type of situation.

For this very reason, reaching out to people to interview for my BA or even people to interview for this book didn't feel as big of a hurdle as before. Don't get me wrong, it's still exhausting sometimes—especially as the occasional introvert that I am—but it's doable, and it's something that I am growing more comfortable doing day after day.

STEP 6: KEEP YOUR NETWORK IN THE LOOP

Now that we've discussed who your network is and how to build your network, let's talk about how to maintain your network. One of the things supervisors, mentors, and professors kept telling me throughout college was to "keep them in the loop." I always responded with a "I'll keep you updated!" yet deep down I questioned if their interest was genuine and how I could possibly keep them in the loop without seeming awkward.

Let me let you in on a little secret: The people in your network genuinely do want to know how you're doing and see all the things you've been up to. How do I know? For one, I've attempted this method of updating mentors on my life, and every time they reply being genuinely excited for me! When they can, they'll even go the extra mile to give me some advice or feedback or offer to help out in whatever way they can.

Second, I have gotten to the point where I have mentored a few students of my own, both through volunteering opportunities and at UChicago, and I always tell them to reach out to me and keep me updated on their lives. Not many do, yet when one of them does it absolutely makes my day. I will go out of my way to either read college application essays, offer insights, or just talk on the phone about an opportunity. The people in your professional or personal circle want to be there to support you, so let them! And the only way they can do this is by knowing what you're up to, how you're doing, and how they can help.

It's also worth mentioning that when you are reaching out to your network, always be genuine. You don't want to be that person who reaches out only when you need something. Reach out just to say hello. Or send a podcast you think they might like. Be there to celebrate them in their own career wins.

STEP 7: FIND MENTORS

Mentorship can single-handedly be one of the biggest ways to help a FLI student navigate the world of higher education. It's important that first-generation, low-income students have someone that they can identify with whether that be similar background or socioeconomic status or even similar career interests. A mentor can offer an additional perspective into majors, classes, and careers. Jayla Galvez had a mentor during college and remembers it as a particularly positive experience.

She explains, "Having a mentor has been an enriching experience, especially since my mentor works in the field that I aspire to work in. As a freshman, it's difficult to know which direction I am supposed to go in, especially since I am the first in my family to choose this type of career, but having a connection with someone in the field has made things a lot clearer."[49]

As a first-generation college student there were many experiences that were new to me. Unlike many of my classmates, I couldn't call home and ask my family how to look for summer internships or how to choose a job. Instead, I had to look for upperclassmen at UChicago who could answer my questions and be there to help me navigate unknown situations.

Mentors in college can be found through a variety of means, including formal mentoring programs or informal relationships. I've had a combination of both. If your college has a structured mentoring program, I would highly encourage you to apply as it's always easier to be assigned a mentor than try to go out and find one yourself. If your college does not have an established mentoring program—or even if it does—it is always beneficial to look for mentors on your own. These can be upperclassmen in your college, faculty, teaching assistants, and eventually, supervisors.

Mentors are people you can go to about anything, from choosing classes to choosing your first job or internship. Some of my mentors have been people I've worked closely with during internships, friends who are now professionals, and staff members. Let's walk through an example of a time I reached out to a mentor and how I went about asking for advice.

---

49   Matthew Hurwitz, "Building a Mentoring Program for First-Generation College Students," Salesforce, March 4, 2020.

I met this person when she was a teaching assistant for High Jump. She is a few years older than me and thus already a few years into the workforce. As I was deciding between two job offers during the spring of my senior year, I reached out to her with the following message:

> Hi! I currently have two job offers on the table and I'm having a hard time deciding between the two. Would you be able to offer any insights on deciding between them, or things I should be looking out for?

Since I'd already built some rapport with her, I texted her a fairly casual and straightforward message. And since she is a part of my network, I'd already been keeping her updated on my job search so my message wasn't out of the blue. She then proceeded to ask me follow up questions about salary, location, and what I wanted to get out my first job. All in all, she provided many good points for me to consider and was a great resource in helping me decide where to accept my first job.

Finding mentors isn't always easy. But when you find the right ones, they can help you work through all kinds of decisions, big and small.

ACTION CHECKLIST
- [ ] Create a running list of professional connections you know and how they might be able to help you in your professional career (some starting points can include professors, upperclassmen, advisors, or previous managers or coworkers).

☐ Before heading to a networking event, nail your "elevator speech": who are you and what are you looking for (internship, full-time position, volunteer opportunity, and anything else).

☐ Write down goals of how you can begin to build and maintain your own network.

☐ Identify what parts of networking might come easily to you and what parts might be harder. How can you work toward becoming more comfortable with the harder aspects? How can you leverage the easier parts?

PART 4

SENIOR YEAR

CHAPTER 10

USING THE POWER
OF SOCIAL MEDIA

———

"In times like these, as a Latina investor and a child of immi-grants, I think it's important to continue to show how we immi-grants, in the words of Lin-Manuel Miranda, get the job done."
—NATHALIE MOLINA NIÑO[50]

Nathalie Molina Niño is an entrepreneur and author of *Leapfrog: The New Revolution for Women Entrepreneurs.* She founded her first start up at age twenty and has since continued her involvement in the investment world and has become an active player in investing in women, particularly in women of color and of underrepresented backgrounds. Yet, even in the midst of her greatest successes, Nathalie never forgets where her journey began and how she, as a

---

50 *Forbes,* "Nathalie Molina Nino: About," Forty Over 40, 2016.

first-generation Latina, had to learn to find her way in a world of whiteness and wealth.

For Nathalie, being a FLI college student meant she had to learn to put herself out there and really form connections with students and professionals alike. Growing up, Nathalie remembers her parents reinforcing how being shy could put her at a disadvantage.

YOU'RE NOT ALLOWED TO BE SHY

She was in the car with her family on the way to a family get-together. She was sitting up extra straight, trying not to wrinkle the new shirt her mom had just bought her. As her parents were talking about relatives she hadn't heard of before, she tried to see if she was tall enough to see herself in the rear-view mirror yet. Nope, not yet. But almost there! Just as she was celebrating the small win, her mom called her name.

"Nathalie, you're going to meet some new aunts and uncles today," her mom said, taking a small pause. "Remember, you're not allowed to be shy. Shy is just another word for rude," she said very matter-of-factly.

Get-together after get-together, year after year, this motto stuck with Nathalie. *You are not allowed to be shy.* She practiced not being shy when she noticed there was a relative in the corner not talking to anyone and went up to them to make conversation. For Nathalie, "Hi, how are you?" became the simplest way to get to know someone and start building relationships with people. When she got to college and started thinking about applying for professional opportunities, she always remembered: *You are not allowed to be shy.* This meant she would do things to stand out and get to know people—like writing them a handwritten note or remembering what they were interested in, like baseball or antique shopping.

Now Nathalie considers these small steps as essential to her journey to learning *the art of becoming a hostess.* She considers herself a hostess in that after years of training, she has become comfortable with making conversation with familiar faces and strangers alike. Regardless of who she may be talking to, she always makes sure they feel welcomed and heard. These skills have come in handy in the world of entrepreneurship and investment, where Nathalie is frequently meeting and partnering with people in a variety of industries. Whenever she walks into a room ready to get to work and network, her mom's voice echoes through her head: *You are not allowed to be shy.*

Without recognizing it, Nathalie's mom was training her to "network" and to connect with people around her. While learning this skill is incredibly beneficial in the professional and academic world, it is usually most commonly found in the upbringing of higher income students. Students growing up in higher income households learn from an early age how to talk to business people and how to put themselves out there. This means that by the time they get to college they are already fluent in the world of power handshakes, business cards, and asking for connections at companies they want to work for.

As FLI students, this becomes our biggest disadvantage. If we don't begin learning these skills and putting them into practice, we run the risk of falling further behind our higher-income peers in terms of job opportunities and professional advancement. Subsequently, it is imperative that as FLI students we both *build* networking skills and *know* where to form professional connections.

REACHING OUT AND BUILDING CONNECTIONS

Success. We all know we want to be "successful," but what exactly does that word mean? And if we don't know what that means for ourselves, how can we work toward it?

Professors, peers, and administrators at predominantly white institutions oftentimes measure success in one of two ways. The first is the prestige of the graduate school you're heading to after graduation. The second is the prestige of the company and the salary of your first job after graduation. No matter how unrealistic you feel like these expectations may be, the fact that your peers all seem to be working toward it makes it feel like you, too, need to be doing so.

Patrick Jamal Elliot—now a diversity and inclusion professional—remembers being an undergraduate student at Claremont McKenna College (CMC) and feeling like the expectation of monetary success sparked a fire in him propelling him to want to be financially successful for both himself and his family.

He remembers thinking, *I have to do whatever it takes to make sure that when I walk across that stage, I walk into something successful for myself.* That was his priority. In order to achieve that, he started leaning heavily on Career Services at CMC. He joined multiple clubs and took advantage of the resources available to him as a student in a small liberal arts school. Patrick was able to meet up with some CMC trustees and leverage their networks, as well as the CMC Alumni network as a whole. For him, these meetups proved invaluable.

He remembers setting up a coffee chat with a CMC alumni to talk about their work in the diversity and inclusion (D&I) space and any advice she had for him. That day, Patrick walked out of his dorm room with more than enough time to find a table at a coffee shop on campus for the meet up. It was a warm and sunny spring morning, when the flowers just started to peek out of their buds.

A few minutes after arriving at the coffee shop and finding the perfect table—shaded and far from a group of students working together—the alumni finally arrived. It didn't take long for them to find similarities in their passion for working in the diversity scene. The alumni, enthralled by Patrick's story and his drive to work in the D&I field, offered to set up an internship for him that upcoming summer. She promised the skills he would learn on the job would be an incredible experience and stepping stone for his career goals.

Now as a corporate diversity and inclusion professional, Patrick attributes his success landing in the industry to alumni like the above who were able to not only guide him in the space, but help him build up his professional skills. Patrick encourages FLI students to leverage their alumni networks as well. While reaching out to people you don't know can be intimidating, these are some points Patrick always included in his outreach efforts and highly recommends.

Meeting up with an alumni or a professional in a field can still be incredibly useful, even if you don't walk away with an internship. Instead, utilize the opportunity to learn more about a particular industry or role. The most important take-away is this: Don't be afraid to voice *how* they can help you, whether that be in navigating a job search, researching a program, or anything in between.

HOW TO REACH OUT
By the time you're an upperclassman, you are becoming more invested in your search for finding internships and job opportunities to help you gauge what you might want to do after graduation. Below are a few tips to help you get started in leveraging your connections and step outside of your comfort zone.

1. If you have a mutual friend or connection in common, mention it!
2. If you don't, don't be afraid to send them a note on LinkedIn or a cold email.
   a. Show interest in their career or current role.
   b. When emailing be sure to answer:
      i. What are your career goals and aspirations?
      ii. How does that organization line up with your aspirations?
      iii. What value can you bring?
3. Be genuine in your questions and how you engage in conversation.

4. When preparing for a meet up be sure you:
    a. Have at least ten questions prepared (You probably won't get through all of them, but it's always good to have backup questions).
    b. Leave with enough time to account for any delays if meeting in person.
    c. Have a few copies of your résumé with you.
    d. Ask for a business card at the end of the conversation!

NETWORKING TOOLS AT YOUR FINGERTIPS

LINKEDIN

As someone who has landed summer internships and this book deal through LinkedIn, it's become more apparent to me than ever that it is a powerful tool to network with people and find professional opportunities. According to *Forbes*, in 2019 LinkedIn had six hundred forty-five million accounts, over thirty million companies, and over twenty million job postings on their platform.[51] I don't know about you, but it definitely sounds like there's ample opportunity on the site. So how do you get a slice of the pie?

1. Include professional media
    a. Make sure your profile and cover photo are professional and up-to-date.
        i. For cheap professional photos, check your campus to see if they offer free LinkedIn photos or ask a friend to take one for you (make sure it's just a

---

51 Ashley Stahl, "How To Use LinkedIn To Your Advantage: Tips To Build Career Success," *Forbes*, January 29, 2020.

headshot of your shoulders and above and includes a plain background).

   b. Use links in your bio and your job descriptions to show examples of your work and the companies and organizations you've worked for.

      i. Use active language that shows what you did. Avoid words like "assisted in." If you were a part of it, you *did* it!

2. Engage with others[52]

   a. Celebrate others' milestones, share interesting posts, and comment in support of the people on your network.

   b. Follow companies you are interested in working for to stay updated on their latest news.

3. Stay connected

   a. Whether it's a previous employer, a coworker, or a recruiter, stay connected on LinkedIn and ensure you are keeping your network updated on your current projects and roles. You never know when a connection is going to come in handy.

4. Use the drop-down menus

   a. Make sure when you're adding a position title or a skill, you utilize the choices on the drop-down menu to ensure the LinkedIn search algorithm is working in your favor.

JOPWELL

According to their About page, Jopwell is "a career advancement platform for Black, Latinx, and Native American

---

52 Ibid.

students and professionals."[53] Jopwell helps companies ensure they are recruiting through a diverse pool of applicants by connecting students with job opportunities. While I have not personally used Jopwell much, I know of a few friends who are heavily involved on the page and attribute it to helping them find roles, a supportive network, and the resources and skills needed to succeed at their internships and jobs.

In addition to connecting students and professionals to job opportunities, Jopwell also offers career advice and networking events to help even the playing field in the professional world for Black, Latinx, and Native American students and professionals. Some of Jopwell's corporate partners include Bain & Company, Goldman Sachs, and NBCUniversal.

RIPPLEMATCH

RippleMatch is an organization that helps match you with job opportunities you may not have known about before. I used this a lot my senior year of college to virtually interview with a lot of different jobs and eventually landed one. RippleMatch's mission is to help candidates from various backgrounds find opportunities they are passionate about. Once you complete their online profile and upload your résumé, they'll "identify opportunities, walk you through interviews, and celebrate with you when you land your dream job."[54] All

---

53 Jopwell, "Who We Are—Jopwell," Jopwell, 2020.

54 RippleMatch, "Jobs and Internships for College and Early-Career Candidates," RippleMatch: Jobs and Internships for College and Early-Career Candidates, 2020.

in all, RippleMatch is a great way to get job opportunities sent to your inbox automatically and know they've already been pre-screened based on what you're interested in, such as industry, location, or salary.

RÉSUMÉS AND COVER LETTERS

If you want to apply to a job or an internship in college, you can anticipate the application will ask you for at least two items: your résumé, and your cover letter. A résumé is a way for your prospective employer to see what your work experience is and what skills you would bring with you to the job. A cover letter is a way for you to explain why you're passionate about an opportunity and why you're the perfect person for the job.

Résumés have a variety of structures depending on industry. If you're in a STEM field you might have publications, symposium presentations, or research experience you want to include in your résumé. Depending on your work experience and the field you're looking to go into, you might include volunteer experience and leadership opportunities. Your résumé does not just have to include paid opportunities. Make sure you edit your résumé depending on the kind of opportunity you are applying for to stand out to a recruiter.

The key to writing a good cover letter is using examples. You are proving to the recruiter reading your letter that you have the experience to be successful in the field because of the work you've already done. Be specific about the responsibilities you had in your previous role(s) and how you executed them. If you can, utilize numbers to emphasize your impact.

It's always a great idea to get a career advisor or a mentor in the field to offer feedback on your letter.

I've included an example of a cover letter and résumé at the end of this chapter to give you a general idea as to what they look like. As a note, résumés vary greatly across industry. I used my résumé as a Public Policy major in college with the aim of landing a corporate opportunity. Connor used his résumé to get into a PhD program.

ACTION CHECKLIST

☐ Identify what kinds of opportunities you are looking for (internships or full-time jobs, location, pay, and anything else).

   ☐ Which people do you know already who are working in the fields you are interested in?

   ☐ What types of extracurriculars or volunteer opportunities have you enjoyed being a part of? Is there a job that utilizes some of those same skills?

☐ Make an appointment at Career Services at your school.

   ☐ Ask a career advisor to help you build your résumé or update it if you already have one.

   ☐ Tell them about the types of internships or jobs you might be interested in and find out where they recommend you to look for opportunities.

   ☐ Ask about an alumni network—is there anyone you can reach out to talk about their career and job?

   ☐ If Career Services isn't as helpful to you, make an appointment with an advisor, professor, or mentor you trust.

☐ Make a game plan for updating your LinkedIn and starting accounts with Jopwell or RippleMatch.

☐ Reach out to people in your network and let them know what kinds of opportunities you are looking for.

JESSICA I. MORA
123 W Devon Ave | Jacksonville, FL 32202| email@gmail.com | 773.123.4567

EDUCATION

University of Chicago   Chicago, IL
Bachelor of Arts in Public Policy   June 2020
- GPA: 3.61/4.0; Dean's List 2017-2020
- Honors: Kimpton Fellow, Odyssey Scholar, Modus Vivendi Society

PROFESSIONAL EXPERIENCE

The Home Depot   Jacksonville, FL
Financial Analyst   August 2020 – Present
- Track marketing email engagement metrics on Tableau and SQL and reported out to 50+ key stakeholders
- Project managed the integration of Salesforce and Acoustic marketing platforms involving migrating over 10k+ contacts, queries, sign up forms, and programs

Capital Group   Los Angeles, CA
The Associates Program (TAP) Intern   June 2019 – August 2019
- Designed and developed an English to French Translation Guide for digital and print marketing materials used to update and expand company's breadth of content for its growing French-Canadian client set
- Organized and facilitated collaboration across legal, marketing and sales teams to standardize language and key terminology across materials to create consistency across organizational communication
- Managed team of 5 interns to plan and conduct research on the next market/industry to be disrupted by the "on demand" business model to support leadership in making more informed strategic business decisions

The University of Chicago Medical Center—Office of Internal Medicine   Chicago, IL
Research Assistant   October 2017 – Present
- Design and execute recruitment plan for Spanish-speaking participants in community violence prevention study
- Regularly conducted literature review of 20+ resources and created quarterly newsletters for 6 health clinics nationwide including developments in diabetes management and personalized care
- Analyzed and derived insights from quantitative data from study on health disparities among Latina patients using SAS and NVIVO software and developed infographics for research team leadership

The University of Chicago Center for Global Health   Intibucá, Honduras
Research Assistant   June 2018 – August 2018
- Conducted health worker surveys via Qualtrics of 120 participants on their health service delivery experiences and overall health outcomes to analyze the effects of decentralized healthcare
- Identified, conducted outreach to, and interviewed 50+ community members, mayors, and health workers to analyze the effects of decentralized healthcare reform
- Analyzed and derived findings from quantitative and qualitative data and presented to 20 leaders and attendees at the Consortium of Universities for Global Health (CUGH) conference

LEADERSHIP EXPERIENCE

High Jump Chicago   Chicago, IL
Special Projects Intern   September 2019 – Present
- Liaison between teaching assistants, teachers, volunteers, and the campus director, facilitating open communication and monitoring project progress to ensure alignment to programmatic goals
- Identify alumni professional development needs and design and execute programming to strengthen alumni engagement and persistence post-graduation

Center for College Student Success, University of Chicago   Chicago, IL
Student Advisory Board Co-Chair   October 2016 – June 2020
- Identify and implement opportunities to improve annual recruiting/onboarding process of 8-10 new board members
- Liaised with CCSS leadership to communicate planning progress and gather leadership direction on key financial, social, and academic issues faced by first-generation, low-income students

SKILLS

Language: Fluent in English, Spanish, and French
Computer: STATA, R, NVIVO, SAS, Tableau, Acoustic, SQL

This is a résumé geared toward corporate and marketing opportunities.

CONNOR SAUCEDA

1234 Example St #1, Los Angeles, CA, 90013 • XXX-XXX-XXXX • email@gmail.com

EDUCATION	**Ph.D. Student, Environmental Engineering** Viterbi School of Engineering University of Southern California	Expected May 2025
	B.S. Environmental Science, University of Chicago Secondary B.A. in Biological Sciences Overall GPA 3.6/4.0	June 2020
EXPERIENCE	**University of Chicago**, Chicago, IL **Research Assistant, Environmental Microbiology** • Conducting phenotypic selection culturing experiments • Cell culturing and genetic screening • Processing samples and fulfilling miscellaneous lab needs	October 2019 – March 2020
	Ben Gurion University, Be'er Sheva, Israel **Research Assistant, Environmental Engineering** • Working on hybrid biofilter water treatment project • Continually adjusting treatment process and engineering design of biofilter • Analyzing effluent levels of nutrients, heavy metals, particulates, organic carbon	July - September 2019
	University of Chicago, Chicago, IL **Research Assistant, Coastal Ecology** • Assisting in stable isotope analysis, mass spectrometry, DIC analysis • Processing samples and fulfilling miscellaneous lab needs • Interpreting data sets	September 2017 - June 2019
	University of Chicago, Chicago, IL **Teaching Assistant, Earth Systems** • Grading classwork for upperclassmen undergraduates and graduate students • Holding office hours for lecture and classwork clarification • Organizing logistics in field trips and lab sessions	April - June 2019
	Columbia University, New York, NY **Research Intern, Marine Science** • Assembling and managing a phytoplankton incubation experiment • Collecting and processing chlorophyll fluorescence, dissolved nutrients, dissolved oxygen, among other samples • Writing a 20-page research paper and giving a symposium poster presentation	June - August 2018
ACTIVITIES	**Marine Biological Laboratory**, Woods Hole, MA **Semester in Environmental Science Student** • Analyzing biogeochemical dynamics of terrestrial and aquatic ecosystems • Estimating biomass and productivity of local ecosystems through field sampling • Running a six-week independent research project with final paper and presentation	September - December 2018
	UChicago Food Recovery Network, Chicago, IL **Board Member** • Coordinating with on-campus dining halls, cafes, and student organizations to recover leftover food to local shelters and food banks • Outreach work on waste-minimizing practices and redirecting leftover food to shelters and food banks • Redistributing short-notice leftover food to campus students and working to address food insecurity on-campus	September 2017 – June 2020
	Wanxiang Group Corporation, Hangzhou, Zhejiang, China **Ambassador Fellow** • Studied Chinese renewable energy technology and policy • Studied extensively at A123 Systems Hangzhou lithium-ion battery factory • Independent research project presented at symposium	June - August 2017
AWARDS, HONORS, SCHOLARSHIPS	USC Diversity, Inclusion, and Access Fellow QuestBridge Scholar Odyssey Scholar University of Chicago Dean's List	2020 2016-2020 2016-2020 2017, 2018, 2019
COMPUTER SKILLS	Python (Intermediate), R (Intermediate), MS Office (Proficient)	
LANGUAGES	English: Native language Spanish: Intermediate (Reading, Writing, Listening, Speaking)	

This is a résumé geared toward PhD programs and research-oriented opportunities.

1234 Example St. #1
Des Plaines, IL 60016
773.123.4567
email@gmail.com

February 4, 2020
RF|Binder
New York City, NY

To Whom It May Concern:
I am a fourth year student at the University of Chicago, majoring in Public Policy and minoring in Romance Languages (Kimpton Fellow) . I am writing to express my interest in the 2020 Associate Program at RF|Binder. I am confident that work experience in various different industries has prepared me to be successful in a role with RF|Binder.

At Capital Group, I worked within the Canadian division on their sales and marketing team. I created an English to French translation guide for all digital and print marketing materials. As such, I tracked discrepancies in language across all materials and then researched best practices from similar asset management companies. I then presented my findings to the legal, compliance, sales, and marketing teams and facilitated conversations on establishing standardized French language for the company.

Throughout my college experience, I have held numerous research assistant roles. During my junior year, I worked under multiple doctors at the UChicago Medical Center and the School of Social Service Administration. As a research assistant I attended weekly team meetings with each team, recruited patients for a study on neighborhood safety, as well as analyzed data on the Honduran Ministry of Health. Having to simultaneously work on different projects meant that I was able to develop effective project management, communication, and time management skills, skills that would be imperative as a part of the 2020 Associate Program at RF|Binder.

As a co-chair for the Center for College Student Success (CCSS) at UChicago, I have had the opportunity to grow my leadership skills. I lead a team of 10 students to plan and execute 1-2 events per quarter. I also have bi-monthly meetings with the Assistant Directors of the CCSS to provide feedback on student programming and to oversee their peer mentoring program that serves over 60 undergraduates. Being a co-chair has allowed me to use setbacks as learning opportunities and receive feedback to better my growing role with the center.

My experience in a variety of industries has equipped me with a diverse toolset that would be beneficial in the 2020 Associate Program. I believe my corporate experience along with my strategic thinking and ability to adapt will allow me contribute meaningfully to a growing company that prioritizes my professional development. I would greatly appreciate the opportunity to talk to you further about my interest in the position. Thank you for your time and consideration.

Sincerely,
Jessica Mora

A cover letter goes in depth on your job experience and why you're the perfect candidate for the job.

About ✎

I am a current Financial Analyst for Home Depot within their marketing B2B team. Most recently, I was a marketing intern for a global asset management company. This role allowed me to not only learn about the application of language across international marketing, but it also gave me an opportunity to lead meetings, be a team lead on a group project, and gain exposure to the investment management industry as a whole.

Throughout my college career, I held numerous research roles that allowed me to gain experience in project design, data collection, and data analysis. Although my roles have been predominantly focused around the health industry, the diverse and broad skill set I have acquired allows me to be successful in other industries. My ability to lead teams, be an independent thinker, and advocate for first-generation low income (FLI) students has proved crucial to being an advisory board chair on The University of Chicago's Center for College Student Success.

I am an avid language learner, currently fluent in Spanish, English, and French. In my free time, I love to travel, volunteer at a variety of local nonprofits, and do acrobatics.

The About section of your LinkedIn should explain what your current role is, where your work experience lies, and what kind of opportunities you are looking for.

Research Fellowship
University of Chicago Center for Global Health
Jun 2018 – Aug 2018 · 3 mos
Honduras

I assisted in the implementation of a third wave of health worker surveys regarding their experiences, perceptions, and attitudes about the health decentralization reform in Honduras. I also interviewed 50+ people including mayors, NGO's, Directors of the Ministry of Health, Regional Health Authority administrators, as well as local health organizations to analyze the effects of the reform beyond the areas of healthcare. These interviews form a part of a bigger research project with the goal of evaluating the effects and impacts of the decentralization reform throughout Honduras.

see less

When you list your work experience on LinkedIn, choose your title from the dropdown menu and include links where possible.

CHAPTER 11

BUDGETING AND PERSONAL FINANCE

"You can be open and people will probably accept you and be understanding, and if not, they're not really worth your time."
—PATRICK JAMAL ELLIOT

For many FLI students, starting college means becoming financially independent from your family. Patrick's mother and grandmother both attended college—thus not making him a first-generation student. Yet, Patrick still remembers figuring out what it meant to be financially independent as an eighteen-year-old from a low-income background.

For him, it ultimately meant holding eight or nine jobs on campus at any given time. He realized early upon arriving at school that the culture of affluence was prevalent, so much so that "it felt like you couldn't experience Claremont McKenna College if you didn't have money in your pocket." Just as the core curriculum was a part of the CMC experience, so was going to the shopping and downtown area and eating out multiple times a week.

In an effort to fit into this culture, Patrick felt like his only option was to work as much as possible. In some ways that worked in his favor because it resulted in him having a lengthy list of experiences to put on his résumé. Yet, as he spent his college career running from one job to the next, he couldn't help but wonder why he felt the need to work so many jobs just for the sake of fitting in socially.

Now looking back, he wishes he could go back to his first year in college and emphasize that it is okay—and in fact, heavily encouraged—to be yourself. The advice he would give himself is simple, "You can be open and people will probably accept you and be understanding, and if not, they're not really worth your time." The advice can seem difficult to act upon, particularly when deciding whether to go out and socialize with the people around you.

To be quite honest, there are times when it seems like everyone is spending their Saturday nights out of town or at some fancy downtown restaurant. When you are feeling this way, it's important you remember that your real friends are those who will want to hang out with you—the *real you*—regardless of whether or not you can afford a $15 entrée.

LOOKING BACK, MOVING FORWARD

During his first two years at Claremont McKenna College, Patrick remembers having a difficult time acclimating to the social scene. While his outgoing personality made it easy for him to make friends, his low-income background meant he couldn't always afford to do the same activities as his friends.

One common outing for CMC students was going into the Village—an area of Claremont known to have small shops and restaurants. When his friends wanted to go out to the Village to grab a bite, Patrick knew he would be spending at least $15 for a meal that he could've gotten for free at one of the on-campus dining halls. In this scenario, some of his friends would offer to pay for him, yet that wasn't something he felt comfortable with. Instead, he would choose to either cover the expense himself or not tag along.

Fast forward to his junior year of college, and the roles changed. Now that Patrick was an upperclassman and a leader on campus, the trips to the Village had become almost second nature. After two years at CMC he had gotten so used to giving in to impromptu trips that it was no longer unusual for him to do so, it was almost normal—as natural as spending a weeknight in the library.

One day, he and a friend were planning an outing to take a study break from classes and extracurriculars. Before Patrick could stop himself, he asked the question that he had dreaded two years prior: "How about the Village?"

His friend took a beat and then candidly replied, "Hey, I can't really afford it."

"Oh! No worries. I got you. You don't have to pay me back," Patrick chimed in.

Silence. It wasn't awkward silence, but Patrick could see that his friend was taking a moment, trying to figure out the right thing to say back. That's when he caught himself. Two years ago, he had felt weird being asked that question, regardless of how well-intentioned it might have been.

Realizing his mistake, Patrick corrected himself, adding, "Why don't we just stay on campus?"

His friend smiled. "Yeah! That sounds good actually."

Now Patrick urges FLI upperclassmen to continue showing empathy and understanding with other FLI students. While they may have overcome certain obstacles or learned to navigate certain scenarios, it is important to be mindful of the fact that not everyone else has. For Patrick, it's crucial to always remember those first two years of college and keep that perspective in mind. When interacting with FLI students in those scenarios, you have two choices:

> *Do you want to be the ally you wish you had? Or do you want to be part of the problem?*

If you ever get in a situation like Patrick, where you get invited to go out when you can't afford it, here are some quick responses that are proven to work:

- I'm bombarded with work today, so I'd prefer to do something on campus. Is it okay if we eat in the dining hall?

- I'm not hungry enough for a meal. Do you mind if we just grab some ice cream instead?
- Why don't we cook something together? I've been meaning to try a new curry recipe!

BUDGETING TERMS

For many students, the word budgeting can seem both daunting and limiting. Many perceive budgeting as something that will hold them back from eating out as often as they want or limit them from treating themselves. However, if done right, budgeting can be freeing. Day to day, you won't have to think about if you can afford to treat yourself to a meal out or if you'll have enough money to send home that month.

Instead, you'll have your income pre-allocated into categories of your choosing, making your day-to-day money decisions much easier to make. In very basic terms, your budget should include three things: your income, your expenses, and your savings. It is important to remember that budgeting is a tool, not an end solution. A budget can vary from person to person, because they have different financial responsibilities they need to account for.

INCOME

When thinking about your income, consider any money that is flowing into your bank account. This can mean a job, any refunds you get from financial aid, or even any birthday money.

EXPENSES

There are two types of expenses: fixed and variable. Fixed expenses are charges that are due on a certain day of the month. They are non-negotiable payments you have to make. Fixed expenses can include tuition payments, rent, utilities, bills, or Wi-Fi. Variable expenses are costs that can change month to month. This can include food, clothing, transportation, textbooks, school supplies, and so on.

SAVINGS

Regardless of whether you're living in dorms—and thus have most of your living expenses taken care of— or if you're living off campus in an apartment, savings should be an important part of your budget. Save as much or as little as you can a month; it doesn't matter. What does matter is that savings is always a part of your budget. You never know when an unexpected expense is going to come up, so you want to make sure you're prepared.

INVESTING

Chances are you'll hear about peers investing in the stock market. A common piece of advice in the investing world is that the best day to start investing is yesterday. This is because investing utilizes "compound interest," meaning that if you keep your money invested long enough, you'll start getting interest paid on interest. Investing means putting your money somewhere with the expectation that it will grow—although it's impossible to say it will always grow just because it has in the past. Where is that "somewhere"?

Below are some common recommended investing strategies for beginners:

- Roth IRA—a tax-advantaged retirement account where you don't get taxed on the return (i.e., profit) you make. The 2021 contribution limit is $6,000.[55] You don't need to have a job to contribute to a Roth IRA.
- 401(k)—a retirement account typically offered through an employer. Usually, employers match a certain percentage of your contributions.
- Mutual funds—a diverse combination of investments sold together. Index funds are a type of mutual fund that follows a particular "index," like the S&P 500.[56]

HOW TO BUDGET

There are many ways to budget and allocate your money. One method that has grown popular over the years is the 50/30/20 budget rule. This rule states that you should spend 50 percent of your income on needs, 30 percent on wants, and 20 percent on savings. Especially when you're in college and don't have a lot of money to work with, the 50/30/20 rule is a great starting point for a budget.

50 PERCENT—*NEEDS*

In your needs category, you should include your fixed expenses as well as things you absolutely need to buy, like

---

55 Andrea Coombes and Tina Orem, "What Is an Individual Retirement Account (IRA)?" NerdWallet, February 2, 2021.

56 Brianna McGurran and Arielle O'Shea, "How To Start Investing: A Guide for Beginners," NerdWallet, December 17, 2020.

groceries, school supplies, textbooks, and transportation. Needs are things you absolutely have to spend money on in order to survive. If you have to contribute to family expenses, that would go here too.

30 PERCENT—*WANTS*

In your wants category, include things like eating out, buying birthday presents for friends, and treating yourself to something like coffee or small gifts. According to Investopedia, "Wants are all those little extras you spend money on that make life more enjoyable and entertaining."[57]

20 PERCENT—*SAVINGS*

In addition to your checking account, you should also have a savings account. For me, it's always been easiest to automate my savings so that every month 20 percent of my income goes directly to my savings without having to think about it. It's always good to start by having your savings someplace where you can access it in case of emergency. By emergency, I mean facing a delay in getting paid for work, or your laptop breaking down, or having to help your family out a little extra one month. Buying a new laptop or a new phone simply because you want one does not count as an emergency. Once you do withdraw money from your emergency fund, it is important to replenish those funds as soon as possible. Once you have enough of an emergency cushion—usually three to

---

57   Eric Whiteside, "What Is the 50/20/30 Budget Rule?" ed. Marguerita Cheng, Investopedia, October 29, 2020.

six months' worth of expenses—you can start putting some of your money into investments.

BUILDING CREDIT

I remember starting college and hearing the buzz about how it was important to start building credit, but I always came back to the same two questions: *What is credit? And why do I need it?*

Your credit score tells people how trustworthy you are with money. The higher the credit score, the better and the more likely you are to be given opportunities that require you to pay something off. The most common example can be paying off a car loan or paying a mortgage on a house. However, it doesn't mean just that. If you're thinking about renting an apartment, they may check your credit score to see if you are likely to pay your rent on time. Phone companies may also check your credit if you want to buy a phone but don't have the money to pay it in full.

One way to start building credit is to become an authorized user on a parent's credit card account. That way you aren't directly applying for a credit card but still get the benefits of having one.[58] You can also apply for your own credit card (once you're eighteen years old), especially for credit cards that are catered toward students, like Discover Student credit cards. It is advised to apply for student credit cards while you are in college, because you are more likely to get approved

---

58   Kali Hawlk, "How To Build Credit as a Student in 5 Steps," Credit Karma, November 4, 2020.

for them. Once you get approved, you need to be sure to do the following with your credit card:[59]

- Pay off your credit card balance *every* month.
- If you can't pay off your full statement balance, pay off the minimum *at least*.
- Don't use more than 10 percent of your credit limit unless you absolutely have to.
- Don't apply for a new credit line (i.e. credit card) frequently.
- Don't close down your longest credit card account, even if you don't use it.
- Even if your credit score isn't in tip top shape already, you can always build it back up by following the items above.

ACTION ITEMS

- ☐ Be mindful of the fact that while you may be in a financial position to start saving and investing, others may not be, and that's totally okay!
- ☐ If you're over the age of eighteen, apply for a credit card and use it responsibly to start building credit.
- ☐ Make a game plan of what to say when you can't afford to go out.
- ☐ Brainstorm ideas on how you can be an ally for FLI students who can't afford to do things you may be able to afford.
- ☐ Make a list of all of your monthly expenses and income and start creating a budget using the 50/30/20 method or any method of your choosing.

---

59 Graham Stephan, "How To Get A PERFECT Credit Score for $0," YouTube Video, October 25, 2019, 18:22.

- [ ] Be sure to analyze and recalibrate your budget every month.
- [ ] When making financial decisions, refer back to your budget!

PART 5

PLANNING FOR LIFE AFTER COLLEGE

CHAPTER 12

FROM FLI STUDENT TO FLI PROFESSIONAL

———

"The great thing about reflection is that it doesn't inherently cost anything, and doesn't necessarily require special equipment, a specific place, or other people. What it does require is open-ness, authenticity, and compassion towards yourself just as you are—along with a working vision for where you would like to go, and who you would like to become. You have everything you need for reflection wherever you are, right here and now."
—ANA MCCULLOUGH[60]

Ana McCullough is one of those people who I'd always heard mentioned throughout my undergraduate career. Students and faculty alike would speak very highly of her, describing how she helped create the largest first-generation, low-income student community through QuestBridge. In technical

---

60 Ana McCullough, "A Note on Reflection from Ana McCullough, Quest-Bridge CEO and Co-Founder," *The Bridge Blog*, January 2, 2015.

terms, QuestBridge is "a powerful platform that connects the nation's brightest students from low-income backgrounds with leading institutions of higher education and further opportunities. [They] are an aggregator of excellence."[61] Yet from my experience, the QuestBridge network can be best described in one word: family. And the family matriarch is Ana McCullough.

When I flew to FLICON, a first-generation, low-income student conference at Stanford, and saw Ana McCullough was the keynote speaker, I quite literally had no words. As she walked on stage and prepared for her speech on that crisp Saturday morning, there was no question that I was standing in the presence of a powerful woman. Yes, she was powerful, but she was also incredibly kind and generous. She is the kind of woman who doesn't leave her communities behind. Instead, she has made it her life goal to bring them up with her.

WHAT DOES IT MEAN TO BE SUCCESSFUL?

As a Stanford college student, Ana was surrounded by many incredibly motivated students— students who would go on to become doctors, lawyers, politicians, and more. Across majors, however, there was a sense among students to achieve a universal definition of "success": Graduate. Find a job. Make six figures. A study from the National Association of Colleges and Employers cites that a college graduate can expect to earn an average of $45,478 after graduation. In 2019,

---

61 QuestBridge, "Mission & Vision," QuestBridge, 2016.

the average salary for the 2019 graduating class was even higher at $53,889.[62]

While college graduates certainly earn a good wage, these statistics make it clear that graduating with a six-figure salary is close to impossible, especially for students coming from low-income and underrepresented backgrounds. Ana remembers being confronted with the harsh reality of what it would mean to be a "successful" Stanford student and, eventually, a Stanford graduate. At the same time, however, she realized that she was unwilling to conform to a mold that didn't seem fulfilling to her.

Ana knew she wanted college to be a place where she could grow and learn as much as possible. She wanted to find ways to better contribute to the world. She wanted to give back to the people and communities she cared about. It was ultimately these priorities that outshined the financial expectation of being a Stanford student.

Halfway through undergrad, Ana decided to come up with her own definition of success and pursue that in place of the traditional definition. She now looks back at that moment and thinks of it as an identity shift of sorts. Instead of feeling like she was on a course to reach a near impossible definition of success, she chose to build her own experience and her own expectations. Ultimately, this is what led her to be so

---

62 NACE Staff, "Average Salary for Class of 2019 Up Almost 6 Percent Over Class of 2018's," National Association of Colleges and Employers (NACE), September 4, 2020.

successful in her pursuit of a more recognizable and universal QuestBridge experience.

In 1994 when Ana McCullough was an undergraduate student and Michael McCullough was a recent graduate, they co-founded QuestBridge as a summer program for low-income high school juniors as a way to help students transition into one of the most pivotal times of their lives: college. One of the areas she found critical to prioritize during the program was reflection time. Based on her own experience of having to define success for herself at Stanford, she encouraged students to think critically about what they wanted their college experience to be like.

Some of the questions she had students reflect on included:

- How can I creatively approach my college education?
- What is my identity as a Quest Scholar? As a student on my college campus? As a member of my family? As a member of my community?
- What professions will enable me to achieve *all* my life goals—including my financial, family, community, and societal goals?
- What does "learning" mean to me?
- What does "being happy" mean to me?[63]

SEEKING OUT NONTRADITIONAL ADVICE

As soon as students arrive on campus they are thrown into a pool of resources they have to swim and sort through.

---

63 Ana McCullough, "A Note on Reflection from Ana McCullough, QuestBridge CEO and Co-Founder," *The Bridge Blog*, January 2, 2015.

Similarly, there is a heavy influx of advice coming from everyone and anyone on campus. Advisors, faculty, teaching assistants, and peers will all be eager to share their own experiences and insights with incoming students. One thing Ana wishes she had realized earlier is that while it's important to be open to *traditional advice* (advice given to all students at large), it's important to know that advice may not be feasible for some students and may look completely different for others.

This becomes especially applicable when thinking about post-graduation plans. While going straight into grad-school may be financially doable for some students, it may not always be an option for first-generation, low-income students. Some FLI students may need to move back to their hometown and live with family and may not be able to afford moving to big expensive cities like Los Angeles, San Francisco, or New York.

When I was looking for a job, I made sure that any job I was considering outside of Chicago, my hometown, included a relocation bonus to help me with moving expenses, as well as a good-enough salary to help me live in a new city where I wouldn't have family around. During the job search process I also reached out to other first-generation alumni to talk to them about factors they considered when choosing their first job and how they weighed living in their hometown or moving away.

Ultimately, it helped a lot more to talk to them, because I knew they made a decision with a background very similar to my own, and I felt like they could provide the most adequate advice for my situation. Some things that might be helpful to think about when you're deciding on post-graduate opportunities include:

- Where do you see yourself living? (Think about weather, proximity to family, lifestyle, and such.)
- What industry do you want to try out?
- How does your salary compare to cost of living?
  - Look at websites like Glassdoor for average salaries. Also ask people in your network for their feedback.
- Is there robust public transportation available, or will you need a car to get around?
- What is important to you in your first job? Some examples can include:
  - Mentorship opportunities
  - Rotational programs
  - A cohort of recent graduates

PREPARING FOR POST-GRAD

Something that is oftentimes overlooked about FLI students is the transition from being a FLI student to being a FLI professional. Being a senior in college and having to navigate what it will mean for you to start a job or go to grad school becomes a challenge of its own. You are forced to realize how your next steps are much trickier to navigate when compared to your peers who have connections at some of the top companies.

Ana encourages students in this stage to consider reaching out to the alumni association at their respective colleges. These alumni are a few stages out in life and may have some valuable insights and advice on how to go about finding your way after graduation. Similar to navigating college as a FLI student, it is important to remember that *you don't have to do it alone.* Just as you are going through something now, it is very likely a previous FLI student has gone through that same experience. So don't be afraid to reach out and start building those connections now.

Of course, in managing these new relationships, it's important to keep a few points in the back of your mind. The first is not to under ask. Sometimes the people you reach out to are willing to help out with more than just a phone call. You could ask them to make a connection for you via email or connect you to a recruiter at their company. Asking for what you need and what you think might be helpful for you is the first step here.

The second step is to trust yourself and your instincts. As a FLI student, you've already gotten so far and overcome so many obstacles. Ana passes along a wise piece of knowledge reassuring FLI students that

> *While it's a vulnerable time to be out in the world on your own, be confident that even if there's a hiccup, you're going to get back on your feet and it's going to be okay. You are not just a survivor, you are a person who has thrived in challenging circumstances. While there may be a lot of things you don't know (yet), there's something deeper that you do have and that is a force to be reckoned with.*

FIRST-GENERATION PROFESSIONAL

One of the things I didn't consider was how tricky the job search process would be as a first-generation, low-income student. When starting my senior year, I already felt like I was behind because a lot of students had started posting job offers on their social media sites. In an effort to get more exposure, I reached out to people in my network and grabbed coffee with them to talk about the industry they worked in, how to make myself a more appealing candidate, and learn about positions that might be available to me after graduation. Getting to meet with so many different people felt like a huge blessing. I was talking to actual working professionals— most of whom were FLI graduates—and getting the inside scoop on how to navigate the professional world.

Now, I would be lying if I didn't reveal how absolutely exhausted I felt during my search. I would find a job I really liked, talk to someone at the company, interview, and then not get the position. Getting rejected along with being surrounded by students who were getting positions at companies like Bain & Company, McKinsey & Company, and Goldman Sachs felt like a lot of pressure. I didn't necessarily want a position at those companies, but I was more jealous of what working at those companies meant: 1) having a job secured *before* even reaching graduation; and 2) knowing you were going to make "good" money after college. As a FLI student, that's really all I wanted. I wanted a job that would pay me well enough so that I would be able to be financially independent from my parents.

While everyone's path is different as to *how* they find jobs, these are some tips that helped me.

FIGURE OUT WHAT YOU'RE LOOKING FOR

1. Is there an industry that appeals more to you?
2. Are you leaning more toward a particular role or a rotational program?
   a. A rotational program will "expose you to different departments in the company, giving you the chance to figure out what you're best at and where in the company you can thrive long-term."[64]
   b. Will you need work-authorization?
   c. What things did you really enjoy doing at your previous internships or jobs? What things didn't you like as much?

UPDATE YOUR LINKEDIN

1. Make sure your LinkedIn has an updated and professional photo of you.
2. Update your LinkedIn with all your previous work experience.
3. Say what kind of opportunities you are looking for in your LinkedIn Bio.
4. Your LinkedIn Bio should include the following information:
   a. Paragraph 1: Who are you (student or position) and what did you do for your most recent role?
   b. Paragraph 2: Summarize your work or volunteer experience as you see fit.
   i. Paragraph 3: Include some fun facts about yourself (language skills, what you like to do in your free time, and anything else).

---

64 "4 Reasons Why You Should Consider a Rotational Program after College," RippleMatch, July 31, 2018.

TAKE ADVANTAGE OF YOUR COLLEGE'S CAREER ADVANCEMENT OFFICE

1. Make regular appointments (at least twice a month) with a Career Counselor.
    i.   Have them review your résumé.
    ii. Talk to them about what you're thinking about for post-grad and ask if they have any suggestions or leads for where to look for positions.

ACTION CHECKLIST

☐ Using the questions outlined in this chapter, reflect on what you want your last year of college to look like. What experiences, connections, relationships, and acquaintances are important to you in this final year?

☐ Begin making a list of what qualities you're looking for in a first job. Once you have an idea, talk it through with your network. Make sure they know what you're looking for.

☐ Make a list of FLI alumni you can reach out to for help with your first job search.
    ☐ How can they best support you, given their area of expertise?
    ☐ Can you shadow them at their work or intern for them during break?

CHAPTER 13

BECOMING A FLI
GRADUATE STUDENT

———

"I am so proud of you because as a first-generation college graduate myself, I know it isn't easy to get to this point. I want you to know that Barack and I are proud of all of you, and we can't wait to see everything you go on to achieve."

—MICHELLE OBAMA[65]

There really is only one reason I decided to go to UChicago, and that reason is circus. When I visited UChicago as a prospective student, my host took me to see a show put on by their circus troupe. I was automatically sold. I wanted to be as graceful as the student flowing and moving through the silks. I wanted to be strong enough to lift myself on the

---

65 ABC News, "Michelle Obama's inspiring message to first-generation college students: 'There are so many people who believe in you,'" *ABC News,* August 16, 2018.

trapeze. I wanted to be brave enough to stand on someone's shoulders and learn acrobatics.

My first year, that was my main goal—learn acrobatics—but the biggest question remained as to how. One day, as I sat in my house lounge attempting to learn the names of my new housemates, I overheard someone say that they had done cheerleading and gymnastics in high school. My eyes automatically widened. *Bingo*! I turned and saw who the voice belonged to, and almost on cue, he did a backflip midair. I decided to go up to him and introduce myself.

"Hi, I'm Jess!"

"I'm Connor!"

"I'm thinking about joining the circus at UChicago. Do you want to come with me?"

Any other person might have found this to be an odd request, but Connor did not. Instead, he smiled and said, "Sure! When?"

Over the next four years Connor and I would spend numerous hours learning acrobatics together. Through sunshine or heavy snow, we always found time to push ourselves to incredible heights.

Since I know I want to go to graduate school eventually, I never hesitate to poke Connor's brain about his experience as a FLI graduate student. He is currently a first year PhD student studying Environmental Engineering at the University of Southern California. Having navigated his way through research and study abroad opportunities, as well as narrowing down his academic interests, Connor has many insights into the world of applying to graduate programs.

THINKING ABOUT GRAD SCHOOL

Connor had always thought about grad school as something he wanted to do after graduation, but it wasn't until after numerous research internships that he confirmed his interest. Each successive internship helped him gain a clearer idea of what his research interests were and guided him to figure out what he was particularly passionate about.

He fondly recalls narrowing down his focus to environmental engineering while working on water treatment for a lab in Israel. He described the experience saying, "I was studying these problems that were happening with the world regarding environmental degradation and climate change and I was very interested in them, but I wasn't interested in just studying them. I was interested in trying to develop solutions."

For those interested in graduate school as an option, Connor heavily suggests gaining research experience early on in their college careers. Whether that job be as a research assistant or a lab tech, Connor attributes his experience on the job for helping him broaden his skillset in lab practices. While there will certainly be students who come into college knowing exactly where their research interests lie and thus get years of experience in one lab, don't feel like you're "behind" because you don't. As a mentor for a graduate application mentorship program, that is something he tries to highlight for prospective graduate students.

He reassures them that each student has their own path, revealing, "On my end, I actually worked, on average, probably six months in five different areas. Even I didn't know exactly what I wanted to go through. Even if you do bounce back and forth, play that as a strength that you have experience in these different fields." As Connor was applying to graduate school, he utilized his experience in different fields and labs to highlight that environmental engineering was the path he had chosen out of all the others. Landing your first research gig is easier said than done, but the key? *Personal connections.*

Connor landed his first research job because one of his friends was working in a lab that was looking to hire new people.

A BALANCING ACT

For many first-generation, low-income (FLI) students, college is a balancing act. They have to juggle homework, extracurriculars, and a job. For students thinking about graduate school, adding a research position is part of their day-to-day as well. In order to keep everything in check, it's important you set your own pace and figure out a schedule that works for you.

For Connor, this meant finding a combination of flexible and tight commitments. His lab job was fairly flexible. "I would usually work two or three days a week at the lab. I would often come in and then stay for a few hours. My advisors weren't even there, but I was doing stuff that I didn't need them around to do," he described.

Connor's other job held a fixed schedule, but he was able to work around it with his classes and other work commitments. While balancing two jobs, schoolwork, and other commitments is a tough act to follow, Connor had his schedule down to a science. He vividly recalls, "It was a lot of going directly from schoolwork grinding to lab grinding. I would teach gymnastics and then I did physics lab from 6 to 9:30 p.m."

BUILDING A TIMELINE

Fall quarter of fourth year is one of the busiest times of your college career. On top of all your usual commitments you are now either applying to jobs, fellowships, or graduate programs. A tip that Connor wishes to impart on all prospective graduate school applicants is this: *the timeline of fall is very crucial.*

Most applications for graduate school are due on either December 1 or December 15. Connor definitely doesn't miss that season where he was having to complete graduate applications in the middle of finals week. It's an understatement to say those two weeks were a lot to handle.

How do you prepare? Connor shares his words of wisdom:

Set aside time when you can. While you may have pressing timelines for assignments, make sure you don't miss any applications for your schools. Keep track of deadlines. Ideally, one would always plan ahead and manage their timeline, but it can be hard to do so when you're juggling so many different commitments. Don't forget how crucial fall quarter is for your future in graduate school.

Start any fellowship applications in the summer. If you can work on them an hour every day, you will thank yourself later. Once you write an essay for a fellowship, you can build off of it for other applications.

Share your essays with others for feedback. Whether that be a friend, an advisor, or a professor, it is always helpful to have someone read through your writing to offer feedback and revisions.

While you don't necessarily need to know your next move right when you get to college, it's important that you begin exploring your interests, especially if you want to go to graduate school. This chapter includes some simple to-dos you can take advantage of if you think graduate school might be for you.

ACTION CHECKLIST
- ☐ Make a list of three people you can reach out to for help landing research opportunities. Some examples can include:
  - ☐ Career advisors
  - ☐ Professors
  - ☐ Research and fellowship advisors
  - ☐ Peers

- [ ] Find a method of time-management and organization that works for you to juggle your responsibilities and commitments. Some handy tools may include:
  - [ ] A planner or journal
  - [ ] Google Calendar
- [ ] As you gain research experience, ask yourself the following questions:
  - [ ] What do I like about my current position? What do I dislike?
  - [ ] What do I enjoy the most about the research I'm working on? What do I like the least?

CHAPTER 14

SPREAD YOUR WINGS AND FLI

———

*"For there is always light. If only we're brave enough to see it.
If only we're brave enough to be it."*

—AMANDA GORMAN[66]

In the beginning of my senior year of college I only had one goal in mind: get a job before graduation. Before fall quarter even started I was already preoccupied with filling out job applications and writing endless cover letters. I kept a steady list of to-dos.

- Cover letter for Rotational Program
- Coffee with a marketing manager
- Mock interview at Career Advancement

———

66 Amanda Gorman, "Watch and Read L.A. Native Amanda Gorman's Inauguration Day Poem," *Los Angeles Times*, January 20, 2021.

As fall quarter came to an end and my to-do list remained as long as ever, it loomed over me that a third of my senior year was almost over. I had been so consumed with my classes, job applications, and my thesis that I had neglected to truly *enjoy* my last year in college. I knew things had to change for winter quarter.

When I headed back to campus after the holidays, I decided I would make time for friends, for myself, and for the campus around me. That winter I had some of the best weeks of my college career. I made it a goal to say "yes" to hanging out with friends more, even if the cold tried to lure me inside.

Trusty bullet journal in hand, I began being more intentional with my day and allotting time to spend with friends. I decided that for each day I would only have three "top" tasks. Once I got to those three tasks, I was allowed to spend time watching Netflix with a face mask on or go for a walk with a friend. Instead of feeling controlled by my to-do tasks, I took control of them and used them as a motivating factor to not feel guilty about taking time for myself.

As a result, winter quarter was filled with many small yet memorable experiences with friends. I went to the grand opening of a Trader Joe's in Hyde Park where I walked into the store with friends to the beat of a marching band. I spent long hours of the night watching the sequel to *To All the Boys I've Loved Before* while eating dumplings. I made pasta from scratch, kneading and rolling dough with a friend of a friend. I dressed up to go to a fancy Vietnamese restaurant downtown for Chicago Restaurant Week.

As COVID-19 hit and my in-person college experience came to an abrupt end these are the moments I held dear to my heart. As I transitioned to a world of break out rooms and taking classes from my bedroom, it was the spontaneous get-togethers I missed the most. On graduation day, I walked away with the memories of all the people who made me who I am. I will always remember those who offered me a cup of tea during moments I was feeling down and those with whom I shared a $1 milkshake to celebrate making it through midterms season.

I hope this book makes you feel more equipped to conquer your college years and that you know you are not alone. Take what resonates with you and put it into action from day one. You'll be surprised at what you'll get out of it if you do. My biggest wish for you, however, is that you don't get so stuck following the action items that you miss out on *experiencing college*. Every so often, don't forget to stop for a breath, take a step back, and appreciate the people and places that surround you.

I promise you, these are the extraordinary memories that will stay with you after graduation.

ACKNOWLEDGMENTS

———

A few years ago I wrote down "write a book" as a bucket list item, never imagining that only three years later I would actually end up publishing one. None of this would have been possible without my expansive support network that was willing to help me in any way possible.

First and foremost, a thank you to God, without whom I would not have been able to push through this process, especially in the middle of a pandemic where there were days when I felt lost, isolated, and afraid.

Thank you to my parents—my mom, my dad, and Tony—for listening to me talk through ideas all while feeding me the most delicious food. A huge thank you to my brother Brandon. I did most of my writing and editing while listening to him play guitar in the next room. There's no better work music than live music. I love you all dearly!

To all my campaign contributors:

Gabe Barrón, Indira Alejandra Cabrera, Karina Pabon, Casey Talbot, Jennifer Foss, Cesar Patiño, Manuel Antonio Diaz, Maria Montesdeoca, Nathan Pietrini, Nydia Monroy, Jocelyn Pérez, Pamela Velazquez, Gabrielle Wimer, Stephanie Chu, Kristin A. Provencher, Bonnie Kanter, Berenice Martinez, Fernanda Ponce, Amanda Lin, Karla Lopez, Carolina Perez, Rahul Kumar, Josselyn Navas, Michelle Lopez, Olivia Stoeckel, Desiree Smith, Billy Lombardo, Bridget Hennessy, Victoria Lansing, Tara Campbell, Bryce Tuttle, Pilar Neumann, Theophyl Kwapong, Milvia Rodriguez, Frances Kelleher, Linda Trey, Guilherme Galhardo, Jose Reyes, Maya Rodriguez, Christian Porras, Nikita Dulin, Edgar Omar Gualoto, Matthew Schuchman, Valeria Ceron, Heidi Novaes, Emily Pardo, Persephone Tian, Rahul Rangwani, Anne Lim, Whitney Beamer, Mayra Velazquez, Patrick Jamal Elliott, Ileana Lopez-Martinez, Lourdes Taylor, Julia Gerdin, Tricia Crimmins, Isaiah Freeman, Ruth Castro, Julia Mariel Attie, Henry Sican, Lia O'Bryan, Zoe' Alexandria Williams, Sydney Jackson, Alexandria Fields, Kate Lorber-Crittenden, Emilio Balderas, Simone Gewirth, Emily Singal, Angel Zhang, David Mendieta, Ryan Waithaka, Mia Kania, Eleanor Maajid, Jeffrey Garcia, Eric Koester, Elizabeth Tran, Brandon Lov, Leah Peluchiwski, Frani O'Toole, Cynthia Guzman, Sidney Eberly, Chorine Adewale, Gwendolyn Gilbert-Snyder, Olga P. Guerrero, Noah Schwartz, Natalie Pontikes, David Morales, Morgan McDougal,William Trlak, Matthew Neumeier Johanna Guzman, Kayla Chapman, Jocelyne Muñoz, Isabela Artola, Gabino Sanchez Jr., Lisette Gonzalez-Flores, Dinah Clottey, Lizeth Garcia, Miles Alsberry, Sabrina Mahmoodi, Riley Nelson, Keirsha Thompson, Lily Zheng, Connor Sauceda, Jennifer Um, Alexandra Moreno, Tyler Stratton, Cynthia Heusing, Scott Rose, Meghan Grover, Georgy Ann, Tammi

Longsjo, Alex Krulewitch, Freyja Brandel-Tanis, Malak Arafa, Simon Ricci, Sara and Lauren Salzmen, Devon Moore, Laurel Elzinga, Jonny Moss, Juan Carlos Archila, Anabel Mendoza, and Anna Zipp.

Words do not suffice to express how much I appreciate you. When I was told I would have to fundraise thousands of dollars to make this book possible, I was unsure how I would actually meet that goal. Yet, you all pre-ordered books, shared my campaign page, and pushed me over my campaign goal. Thank you!

Thank you to all of my beta readers:

Nydia Monroy, Pamela Velazquez, Anabel Mendoza, Whitney Beamer, Yessica Vargas, Josselin Perez, Emily Kim, and Malak Arafa.

Your feedback was invaluable in helping make this book the most useful for FLI students.

To all my interviewees:

Daniel Flores, Jeffrey Garcia, Asennette Ruiz, Dr. Vijay Pendakur, Diestefano Loma, Bonnie Kanter, Sandra Bustamante, Guillermo Camarillo, Maddy Molina, Xiomara Contreras, Nathalie Molina Niño, Patrick Jamal Elliott, Ana McCullough, and Connor Sauceda.

Thank you for being so willing to take time out of your day to share your experiences with me about being a FLI student or being in the higher education space. Your interviews were crucial in helping me capture the intricacies and differences in experience even within the FLI community.

To my High Jump family:

Who would have known that a summer program I did in seventh and eighth grade would become my biggest support system in high school, college, and beyond. Thank you for always having my back and never being too busy to sit to grab coffee. A huge thank you to Nate and the rest of the High Jump faculty and staff, the Alumni council, and the numerous alumni who are always available to lend a hand.

To the Center for College Student Success (CCSS):

Devon, Jeremy, and Bonnie, thank you for making my first year at UChicago the best it could have ever been. I never felt like someone didn't have my back, because you all were always there to listen and guide me to the right resources. I am where I am today because of all of your guidance.

Talaya and José—you both came into the CCSS and put your hearts and souls into making the office a place that was inclusive to all FLI students and not just Odyssey Scholars. Thank you for always being a resource and continuing to foster a tightknit and supportive environment on campus.

To my amazing editors:

Jordan Waterwash—you were the first one to hear the stories I wanted to share in this book. Thank you for guiding me through the process of brainstorming, writing stories, and crafting chapters. Your advice and insights helped me stick to my instincts and make sure this book was what I wanted it to be.

Kendra Kadam—your advice and weekly check-ins kept me on track week to week. It was easy to stay excited and not feel overwhelmed with the process when you always started every call with a smile. You were a constant support during writing, editing, and especially during crowdfunding.

I couldn't have gotten through this process without either of you!

APPENDIX

——

INTRODUCTION

American College Personnel Association. "The 'Thriving Quotient':
A New Vision for Student Success," May 2010. https://www.
wellesley.edu/sites/default/files/assets/departments/studentlife/
files/thriving_overview.pdf.

Chetty, Raj, Nathaniel Hendren, Patrick Kline, and Emmanuel
Saez. 2014. "Where is the Land of Opportunity: The Geography
of Intergenerational Mobility in the United States." Quarterly
Journal of Economics 129 (4): 1553–1623.

Jack, Anthony Abraham. "Culture Shock Revisited: The Social
and Cultural Contingencies to Class Marginality." Sociological Forum, 2014. https://scholar.harvard.edu/anthonyjack/
publications/culture-shock-revisited-social-and-cultural-con-
tingencies-class-marginality.

US Department of Education. "Fulfilling the Promise, Serving
the Need: Advancing College Opportunity for Low-Income
Students." March 2016.

CHAPTER 1

Hough, Lory. "Poor, but Privileged." *Harvard Ed. Magazine*, 2017. https://www.gse.harvard.edu/news/ed/17/05/poor-privileged.

Jack, Anthony Abraham. *The Privileged Poor: How Elite Colleges Are Failing Disadvantaged Students.* Cambridge, MA: Harvard University Press, 2019.

Tchen, Tina. "First Lady Michelle Obama: 'I'm First.'" *National Archives and Records Administration.* February 5, 2014. https://obamawhitehouse.archives.gov/blog/2014/02/05/first-lady-michelle-obama-i-m-first.

The Community Initiative. "What Is FGLI?" *Yale University.* 2020. https://fgli.yalecollege.yale.edu/our-community/what-fgli.

CHAPTER 2

Aisch, Gregor, Amanda Cox, Kevin Quealy, and Larry Buchanan. "Economic Diversity and Student Outcomes at the University of Chicago." *The New York Times.* January 18, 2017. https://www.nytimes.com/interactive/projects/college-mobility/university-of-chicago.

American Academy of Arts and Sciences. "Getting into College." A Primer on the College Student Journey: American Academy of Arts and Sciences, September 2016. https://www.amacad.org/publication/primer-college-student-journey/section/6.

Central Piedmont Community College. "Opportunity Scholars Program." Opportunity Scholars Program, Central Piedmont

Community College, 2020. https://cpcc.academicworks.com/
opportunities/5555.

Deardorff, Julie. "Tony Jack on Diversity: 'Access Ain't Inclusion.'"
Northwestern University: School of Education & Social Policy. October 29, 2019. https://www.sesp.northwestern.edu/
news-center/news/2019/10/when-youre-a-poor-student-on-a-
rich-campus.html.

Chetty, Raj, Nathaniel Hendren, Patrick Kline, and Emmanuel
Saez. "Where Is the Land of Opportunity? The Geography of
Intergenerational Mobility in the United States." NBER Working Paper Series. National Bureau of Economic Research. January 2014. https://www.nber.org/system/files/working_papers/
w19843/w19843.pdf.

Jack, Anthony Abraham. "Culture Shock Revisited: The Social
and Cultural Contingencies to Class Marginality." Sociological Forum, 2014. https://scholar.harvard.edu/anthonyjack/
publications/culture-shock-revisited-social-and-cultural-con-
tingencies-class-marginality, 453-475.

The Patchwork Feminist, 11, "First and Foremost," by host Lyric
Swinton, aired November 2019 on Garnet Media Group. https://
www.garnetmedia.org/page/patchwork-feminist.

Swinton, Lyric. "What I Have Learned as a First-Generation
College Student." Filmed December 5, 2018 at TEDxUofSC,
Columbia, SC. Video, 1:51-2:04. https://www.youtube.com/
watch?v=VRVG7kjvw7g.

Tough, Paul. *Years That Matter Most: How College Makes or Breaks Us.* Chicago, IL: Houghton Mifflin Harcourt, 2019.

CHAPTER 3

ABC News. "From Michelle Obama's humble Chicago upbringing to the White House: Part 1," YouTube. November 11, 2018, https://www.youtube.com/watch?v=eox7hIzoXQ8.

Blackwood, Leighann. "14 Encouraging Life Quotes from Writer and Artist Morgan Harper Nichols." Medium. August 29, 2019. https://medium.com/@ohleighann/14-encouraging-life-quotes-from-writer-and-artist-morgan-harper-nichols-177cedfac947.

Bridges, Frances. "Michelle Obama Shares Advice with First-Generation College Students at Beating the Odds Summit." *Forbes.* July 24, 2019. https://www.forbes.com/sites/frances-bridges/2019/07/24/michelle-obama-shares-advice-with-first-generation-college-students-at-beating-the-odds-summit/.

Jack, Anthony Abraham. "For Students Who Grew Up Poor, An Elite Campus Can Seem Like a Sea of Wealth and Snobbery." *Quillette.* August 24, 2019. https://quillette.com/2019/08/24/for-students-who-grew-up-poor-an-elite-campus-can-seem-like-a-sea-of-wealth-and-snobbery/.

Jack, Anthony Abraham. *The Privileged Poor: How Elite Colleges Are Failing Disadvantaged Students.* Cambridge, MA: Harvard University Press, 2020.

Tchen, Tina. "First Lady Michelle Obama: 'I'm First.'" *National Archives and Records Administration.* February 5, 2014. https://obamawhitehouse.archives.gov/blog/2014/02/05/first-lady-michelle-obama-i-m-first.

Tough, Paul. *Years That Matter Most: How College Makes or Breaks Us.* Chicago, IL: Houghton Mifflin Harcourt, 2019.

CHAPTER 4

Tough, Paul. *Years That Matter Most: How College Makes or Breaks Us.* Chicago, IL: Houghton Mifflin Harcourt, 2019.

CHAPTER 5

Almeida, Daniel J., Andrew M. Byrne, Rachel M. Smith, and Saul Ruiz. "How Relevant Is Grit? The Importance of Social Capital in First-Generation College Students' Academic Success." Journal of College Student Retention: Research, Theory & Practice. June 2019. https://doi.org/10.1177/1521025119854688.

Nadworny, Elissa. "College Students: How To Make Office Hours Less Scary." NPR. October 5, 2019. https://www.npr.org/2019/10/05/678815966/college-students-how-to-make-office-hours-less-scary.

Nunez, Vivian. "Self-Advocacy Is a Learned Skill." *Forbes.* June 17, 2016. https://www.forbes.com/sites/viviannunez/2016/06/17/self-advocating-is-a-learned-skill/?sh=1b6e653c7f14.

Walter, Ekaterina. "30 Powerful Quotes on Failure." *Forbes.* January 3, 2018. https://www.forbes.com/sites/ekaterinawalter/2013/12/30/30-powerful-quotes-on-failure/?sh=3b-3da94a24bd.

CHAPTER 6

Canning, Elizabeth A., Jennifer LaCosse, Kathryn M. Kroeper, and Mary C. Murphy. "Feeling Like an Imposter: The Effect of Perceived Classroom Competition on the Daily Psychological Experiences of First-Generation College Students." *Social Psychological and Personality Science* 11, no. 5 (July 2020): 647–57. https://doi.org/10.1177/1948550619882032.

Jack, Anthony Abraham. *The Privileged Poor: How Elite Colleges Are Failing Disadvantaged Students.* Cambridge, MA: Harvard University Press, 2020, 182.

Loma, Diestefano. "What Every First-Gen Student Needs To Know about Attending a Predominately White Institution." Education Post. May 20, 2019. https://educationpost.org/what-every-first-gen-student-needs-to-know-about-attending-a-predominately-white-institution/.

CHAPTER 7

Jack, Anthony Abraham. *The Privileged Poor: How Elite Colleges Are Failing Disadvantaged Students.* Cambridge, MA: Harvard University Press, 2020, 19.

McClenney, Kay, C. Nathan Marti, Courtney Adkins. "Student Engagement and Student Outcomes: Key Findings from CCSSE Validation Research." *Community College Survey of Student Engagement* (2007).

CHAPTER 8

Camarillo, Guillermo. Facebook. July 18, 2016. https://www.facebook.com/permalink.php?story_fbid=1104491926288019&id=100001816657229.

Camarillo, Guillermo. "Why Poor College Kids Like Us Need To Start Asking for the Help We Need." Education Post. May 13, 2017. https://educationpost.org/why-poor-college-kids-like-us-need-to-start-asking-for-the-help-we-need/.

Chicago Latinx Scholars. Facebook. December 21, 2016. https://www.facebook.com/groups/1814656598776706/about.

Elkins, Kathleen. "29 Percent of Americans Are Considered 'Lower Class'-Here's How Much Money They Earn." CNBC. September 30, 2019. https://www.cnbc.com/2019/09/28/how-much-the-american-lower-class-earns.html.

Espinosa, Lorelle L., Jonathan M. Turk, Morgan Taylor, and Hollie M. Chessman. "Race and Ethnicity in Higher Education: A Status." *Report*. Washington, DC: The American Council on Education, 2019.

Hess, Abigail Johnson. "College Grads Expect to Earn $60,000 in Their First Job-Here's How Much They Actually Make." CNBC. February 20, 2019. https://www.cnbc.com/2019/02/15/college-grads-expect-to-earn-60000-in-their-first-job——few-do.html.

Kerry, Leushel. "George Westinghouse College Prep 2019-2020 School Profile." George Westinghouse College Prep, 2020.

https://www.newwestinghouse.org/pdf/GWCP_School_Pro-
file_2019-2020.pdf.

Rodriguez, Laura. "Against All Odds, Son of Undocumented Parents Goes from Little Village to Stanford University." *Chicago
Tribune*. February 5, 2016. https://www.chicagotribune.com/
hoy/ct-hoy-8553110-little-village-stanford-university-story.
html.

Quintana, Chris. "More Latino Students than Ever Are Trying to Get Their Degree, but It's Fraught and Costly." *USA
Today*. Gannett Satellite Information Network. May 24, 2020.
https://www.usatoday.com/in-depth/news/nation/2020/01/06/
more-hispanic-students-than-ever-go-college-but-cost-
high/2520646001/.

CHAPTER 9

American Association of Medical Dosimetrists. "Why Networking
Is Important." American Association of Medical Dosimetrists,
2021. https://www.medicaldosimetry.org/career-services/
why-networking-is-important/.

High Jump. "High Jump Mission." High Jump, 2021. https://high-
jumpchicago.org/about/mission/.

Hurwitz, Matthew. "Building a Mentoring Program for First-Generation College Students." Salesforce. March 4, 2020. https://
www.salesforce.org/blog/building-a-mentoring-pro-
gram-for-first-generation-college-students/.

CHAPTER 10

Forbes. "Nathalie Molina Nino: About." Forty Over 40, 2016. https://fortyover40.com/2017-honorees/nathalie-molina-nino/.

Jopwell. "Who We Are—Jopwell," 2020. https://www.jopwell.com/who-we-are.

RippleMatch. "Jobs and Internships for College and Early-Career Candidates." RippleMatch: Jobs and Internships for College and Early Career Candidates, 2020. https://ripplematch.com/.

Stahl, Ashley. "How To Use LinkedIn To Your Advantage: Tips To Build Career Success." *Forbes.* January 29, 2020. https://www.forbes.com/sites/ashleystahl/2020/01/29/how-to-use-linkedin-to-your-advantage-tips-to-build-career-success/#4d-041d8a4035.

CHAPTER 11

Coombes, Andrea, and Tina Orem. "What Is an Individual Retirement Account (IRA)?" NerdWallet, February 2, 2021. https://www.nerdwallet.com/article/investing/learn-about-ira-accounts.

Hawlk, Kali. "How To Build Credit as a Student in 5 Steps." Credit Karma. November 4, 2020. https://www.creditkarma.com/credit-cards/i/how-to-build-credit-as-a-student.

McGurran, Brianna and Arielle O'Shea. "How To Start Investing: A Guide for Beginners." NerdWallet. December 17, 2020.

https://www.nerdwallet.com/article/investing/how-to-start-investing.

Stephan, Graham. "How To Get A PERFECT Credit Score for $0." YouTube Video. October 25, 2019. 18:22.

Whiteside, Eric. "What Is the 50/20/30 Budget Rule?" Edited by Marguerita Cheng. Investopedia. October 29, 2020. https://www.investopedia.com/ask/answers/022916/what-502030-budget-rule.asp.

CHAPTER 12

McCullough, Ana. "A Note on Reflection from Ana McCullough, QuestBridge CEO and Co-Founder." *The Bridge Blog.* January 2, 2015. https://thebridgeblog.org/2015/01/02/a-note-on-reflection-from-ana-mccullough-questbridge-ceo-and-co-founder/.

NACE Staff. "Average Salary for Class of 2019 Up Almost 6 Percent Over Class of 2018's." National Association of Colleges and Employers (NACE). September 4, 2020. https://www.naceweb.org/job-market/compensation/average-salary-for-class-of-2019-up-almost-6-percent-over-class-of-2018s/.

QuestBridge. "Mission & Vision." QuestBridge, 2016. https://www.questbridge.org/about/mission-and-vision.

"4 Reasons Why You Should Consider a Rotational Program after College." RippleMatch. July 31, 2018. https://ripplematch.com/journal/article/4-reasons-why-you-should-consider-a-rotational-program-after-college-84b6fd85/.

CHAPTER 13

ABC News. "Michelle Obama's inspiring message to first-generation college students: 'There are so many people who believe in you.'" ABC News Network. August 16, 2018. https://abcnews.go.com/GMA/News/michelle-obamas-inspiring-message-generation-college-students-people/story?id=57144691.

CHAPTER 14

Gorman, Amanda. "Watch and Read L.A. Native Amanda Gorman's Inauguration Day Poem." Los Angeles Times. Los Angeles Times, January 20, 2021. https://www.latimes.com/world-nation/story/2021-01-20/watch-and-read-amanda-gormans-inauguration-day-poem.